# THE
# *Sacred Path*
# COMPANION

## A Guide to Walking the Labyrinth to Heal and Transform

*To the Congregation of Grace Church Blessings! Lauren Artress November 15, 2015*

# Lauren Artress

Riverhead Books
New York

**THE BERKLEY PUBLISHING GROUP**
**Published by the Penguin Group**
**Penguin Group (USA) Inc.**
**375 Hudson Street, New York, New York 10014, USA**
Penguin Group (Canada), 90 Eglinton Avenue East, Suite 700, Toronto, Ontario M4P 2Y3, Canada
(a division of Pearson Penguin Canada Inc.)
Penguin Books Ltd., 80 Strand, London WC2R 0RL, England
Penguin Group Ireland, 25 St. Stephen's Green, Dublin 2, Ireland (a division of Penguin Books Ltd.)
Penguin Group (Australia), 250 Camberwell Road, Camberwell, Victoria 3124, Australia
(a division of Pearson Australia Group Pty. Ltd.)
Penguin Books India Pvt. Ltd., 11 Community Centre, Panchsheel Park, New Delhi—110 017, India
Penguin Group (NZ), cnr Airborne and Rosedale Roads, Albany, Auckland 1310, New Zealand
(a division of Pearson New Zealand Ltd.)
Penguin Books (South Africa) (Pty.) Ltd., 24 Sturdee Avenue, Rosebank, Johannesburg 2196,
South Africa

Penguin Books Ltd., Registered Offices: 80 Strand, London WC2R 0RL, England

While the author has made every effort to provide accurate telephone numbers and Internet addresses
at the time of publication, neither the publisher nor the author assumes any responsibility for errors, or
for changes that occur after publication. Further, publisher does not have any control over and does not
assume any responsibility for author or third-party websites or their content.

First Riverhead trade paperback edition: March 2006

Library of Congress Cataloging-in-Publication Data

Artress, Lauren, 1945–
    The sacred path companion : a guide to walking the labyrinth to heal and transform /
Lauren Artress.
        p. cm.
    ISBN 1-59448-182-2
    1. Labyrinths—Religious aspects.    2. Spiritual life.    3. Spiritual healing.    I. Title.
    BL325.L3A76 2006
    203'.7—dc22                                                                2005051041

PRINTED IN THE UNITED STATES OF AMERICA

10   9   8   7   6   5

Most Riverhead Books are available at special quantity discounts for bulk purchases for sales promotions,
premiums, fund-raising, or educational use. Special books, or book excerpts, can also be created to fit
specific needs.

For details, write: Special Markets, The Berkley Publishing Group, 375 Hudson Street, New York, New
York 10014.

# Contents

PART TWO:

# Specific Uses for Healing and Transformation

# Acknowledgments

I have had the privilege of listening to people's labyrinth experiences since 1991. I have taught many workshops, lectured to hundreds in the yearly Veriditas program "Walking a Sacred Path" in Chartres, France, and traveled internationally meeting thousands of men and women. All of you whom I have met and everyone involved directly or indirectly in the Labyrinth Movement have, in some way, influenced this book. Thank you for your candor, sharing your experiences, and your honest responses. You have been my teachers.

I am grateful that Grace Cathedral has been a creative laboratory in my life. Under the leadership of Alan Jones, dean, and William Swing, bishop of California, this vibrant openhearted community is a beacon of light to the world.

I give thanks for the Veriditas board of directors: Jo Ann Mast, Marge McCarthy, Terri Holbrooke, Gary Petersen, the late Melissa Postnikoff, and consultants Barbara Ludlum and Lisa Steckley, as well as those who have served in the past—Mary Davidson, Ellen McDermott, Ann Eichhorn, Bill Garrow, Dixie Horning—and so many others who have helped guide Veriditas, the Voice of the

Labyrinth Movement. Thanks to the many Veriditas donors who have supported this work all these years.

I gratefully acknowledge my publisher, Riverhead, and my editor, Jake Morrissey, for his friendship, expertise, and ability to keep things on track.

I give thanks for my friends Barbara Hartford, Alan Briskin, Rebecca Westerfield, Adrienne and Marge Vincent, Ann McCoy, Renate Stendahl, and the Larks group—Susana McCall, Whitney Roberson, and Lynne Ehlers—which meets monthly for our chicken dinner.

I give special thanks to Judy Powell for her guidance and abiding friendship, Margie Adam for her expertise in editing, deep listening, and friendship, and to Tom Keelan, Adrienne Morello, and Pamela Oviatt for their hard and steadfast work in the early stages of Veriditas.

# Introduction

*One of the oldest images of the mystery of life, death, transformations and return is the labyrinth . . . in which we fear to lose ourselves.*

—Edward C. Whitmont, *The Symbolic Quest*

When I began to introduce the labyrinth one of the first questions I was asked was: What do you do in the labyrinth? I didn't take this question very seriously at first. But as the body of labyrinth work developed, this question became a guideline to teach how to use the labyrinth as a practice to heal and transform our lives.

I began to speak about the profound powers of the Medieval Eleven-Circuit Labyrinth in 1992. A year earlier, as canon for Special Ministries at Grace Cathedral in San Francisco, I had arrived at the portals of Chartres Cathedral with five friends from Grace Cathedral, to see for myself the healing powers of this ancient symbol. After physically removing the chairs covering it, we were able to walk the labyrinth inlaid in the floor. Little did I know I was about to embark on an odyssey of teaching, lecturing, and guiding a meditative and insight-filled process that profoundly changed my life and touched many other lives just as significantly.

A few years after I began to teach this meditative process, I came across the work of Linda Sussman, author of *The Speech of the Grail: A Journey toward Speaking That Heals and Transforms*. Through her work with the medieval story of Parzival, I began to understand the labyrinth as a form of the Grail. Sussman names three characteristics of the Grail: first, it meets you where you are; second, it gives you what you need; and last, it "nurtures an invisible web of relationships that connect individual destiny to service of others and to the earth."[1] These three elements are what the labyrinth can bring to all of us.

There are many reasons to walk a labyrinth—solace, strength, clarity, celebration, insight, to quiet the mind, to solve a problem—but the most fascinating result, on which I have based my work, is the ability of the Medieval Eleven-Circuit Labyrinth to ignite seekers' latent potential and find an avenue for its expression in the world. The labyrinth is a Grail in that it connects individual destiny to service in the world. The way the Spirit evokes this to unfold in our lives is an intriguing creative process that I enjoy guiding.

Another intriguing aspect of the Grail is that no one owns it. This is also true of the great archetypal labyrinths.[2] These labyrinths are blueprints for transformation. They release a psychospiritual process of discovery that organically unfolds in our lives. Spirit guides this process. Though I never would have compared the labyrinth to a Grail in the "early days"—and I am still a bit uncomfortable speaking so publicly about the labyrinth in this way—the gifts that I see taking root in people who embrace a practice of labyrinth walking far outweigh the hidden safety of silence.

The labyrinth that is my heart song is the Medieval Eleven-Circuit Labyrinth replicated in Grace Cathedral from the floor of Chartres Cathedral. When I refer to the labyrinth, I am picturing this pattern in my mind. This labyrinth opens the door to our inner symbolic world. When we touch this fountain of images with a quiet, receptive mind, it restores and energizes us. Because we are bombarded with noise and images coming at us from the outside, we can lose our capacity for reflection within. We can feel parched inside and our imaginations dry up and stop functioning. We are drawn to the labyrinth because it replenishes our imaginations and restores our natural rhythms. The literal path becomes the symbolic path leading us through life. The turns speak to us as we move through the turns in our lives. We can arrive at the labyrinth feeling utterly empty and confused and leave feeling calm with a renewed sense of purpose. Our pain becomes *the* pain we all share as human beings. We sense our connection to the deeper Mystery unfolding around us.

*Divinity is like a wheel, a circle, a whole.*
—Hildegard of Bingen

I had a wordless intuitive understanding within me when I first placed the newly painted canvas labyrinth in the nave of Grace Cathedral on December 30 and 31, 1991. When the public began to walk it on a regular basis in March 1992, this intuition instructed me to listen—listen to the experiences people had in the labyrinth. Some people shared fragments of insight, others complete stories. The methods for walking the labyrinth I describe in this book developed over the years from these observations. Out of these experiences a pattern became visible—a map—that I have more recently been calling the three Rs (releasing, receiving, and reflection).[3] I discuss these in chapter 3, "The Art of Labyrinth Walking."

My work is not an effort to recapture how it was walked in the Middle Ages. Though we have some confirmation that the labyrinth in Chartres Cathedral was walked at that time, we do not know how it was understood. Most likely it was symbolic of the journey to God. Nor do we know *how* our ancestors walked it. Did they use the same inward path to return, or did they walk out the back of the center? Did they crawl it on their knees? We may never know this because the records from Chartres Cathedral were destroyed during World War II.

The publication of *Walking a Sacred Path: Rediscovering the Labyrinth as a Spiritual Tool* in 1995 put all that I learned—the background, the history, and the rationale for reclaiming the labyrinth as a spiritual practice—into one book. Since then, as I've learned and understood more about the labyrinth, my ideas have deepened and crystallized, so in some way I consider this a sequel to *Walking a Sacred Path*. The labyrinth adds a dimension to my work as a transpersonal psychotherapist, Episcopal priest, life coach, and spiritual director I could not have imagined or achieved on my own.

But this book is more than a sequel. It's designed to be a quick, easy-to-read resource to encourage people to develop their own practice of labyrinth walking. It need not be read cover to cover. Part 1, "The Practice of Walking the Labyrinth," contains all one needs to know about using the labyrinth and serves as a guide for newcomers to the practice. It begins with "Four Guidelines to Gauge Your Spiritual Growth" to emphasize the fruits of having a practice in our lives. In "Lessons of the Labyrinth," I discuss what the labyrinth can teach us. Following that is "The Art of Labyrinth Walking," which serves as "the basics" to meditative walking written for anyone new to the labyrinth. The last chapter of part 1, "Applications," makes specific suggestions for using the labyrinth as a spiritual practice. My hope is that here the experienced labyrinth walker will discover new insights into using this profound blueprint of transformation.

Part 2, "Specific Uses for Healing and Transformation," has two purposes. First, it is designed to take labyrinth walkers deeper into the process. In *Walking a Sacred Path* I relied on the stories that people shared with me to organize this information under three areas: healing, shadow work (earlier called self-knowledge), and soul assignment (earlier called co-creation). In my lectures since then, I have added a fourth category—initiatory rituals. It is important to note that there are other methods, besides meditative walking, of walking the labyrinth.[4] Ritual and ceremony are another way to use the labyrinth—for instance, the processional method, which I explain in chapter 9, "Initiatory Rituals."

Part 2 is also designed to foster personal reflection. "Start Where You Are" provides a way to discern where you are on your journey. This will be especially important for those who want to use this book as a guide during a specific period in their lives. After you read this chapter, you may want to choose the chapter on healing, shadow work, soul assignment, or initiatory rituals depending upon your life circumstances. Another way to use this book is to browse through the exercises until you find one that attracts your attention.

The methods in this book can be applied and modified to work with any labyrinth. They can also extend beyond labyrinth walking into other practices in your life that nurture a quiet mind, nonjudgmental witnessing, and an open-ended receptive approach.

The conclusion offers a broader picture of an authentic spirituality. I am often asked, How does the labyrinth work? Why does it have such a profound effect on so many people? What are the elements that evoke the

*The new temple of initiation is the world itself.*
—Robert Sardello

unfolding of the human spirit through the labyrinth? These questions go to the heart of archetypal labyrinths and into the core of the Mystery itself. We can rely on the Grail myth to help us find the answer, so I have woven it in throughout this book.

"The new temple of initiation is the world itself"[5] and all of us are initiates because we are citizens of planet Earth. We need peace within through nurturing a quiet mind. We need a place free from our addictions to steep ourselves in sacred teachings through art, music, creative flow, and wisdom stories. Only then can we let go of our armor to receive the beauty of our magnificent natural world and the invisible Spirit working with us to heal and transform.

# PART ONE

# The Practice of the Labyrinth

*There is nothing so wise as a circle.*

—Rainer Maria Rilke

In modern culture, we need to be able to quiet our minds. We have enormous pressures on us. The media spend billions of dollars a year to grab our attention and focus it on a dizzying array of products. If you are unsure of what you want to think about and unclear about how you want to focus your mental, emotional, spiritual energy, you are vulnerable to manipulation from the media and from advertising in all forms.

Even more disturbing, it's the media's stated goal to break up our attention spans into bite-sized pieces of ten to thirty seconds. Is it any wonder that children as well as adults are having trouble focusing? Unless you can create an inner sanctuary, a special chamber within, where you can be with yourself, slow things down, and direct your thoughts toward what nourishes you in body, mind, and Spirit, you will be starving for meaning and purpose in your life. The labyrinth can help you create this inner chamber; it can provide a touchstone to return to when you need to remember who you are and where and with whom you stand.

Quieting my mind has been a challenge, and remains so to this day. I know that I am not alone when I call myself a "failed meditator." Whenever I give a talk, this statement is met by a chuckle of recognition. My mind is a shining example of what the Buddhists call "monkey mind." It is as if I have a hyperactive monkey jumping from tree to tree—hemisphere to hemisphere—in my brain. Few things quiet this monkey. This is a very pertinent issue for many of us.

In the West, we define meditation very narrowly. Most meditation techniques come from one of two sources: the monastic traditions of Europe or the Eastern methods transplanted to the West. The Beatles, whose return from India clean and sober received international attention, opened the door to teachers from the East. Both sources encourage sitting meditation.

Those who are familiar with Anthony de Mello's work know that his stories capture a dialogue, such as this one, between a Master and his pupils:

> The Master was asked: "What is spirituality?"
>
> He said, "Spirituality is that which succeeds in bringing one to inner transformation."
>
> "But if I apply the traditional methods handed down by the masters, is that not spirituality?"
>
> "It is not spirituality if it does not perform its function for you. A blanket is no longer a blanket if it does not keep you warm."
>
> "So spirituality does change?"
>
> "People change and needs change. So what was spirituality once is spirituality no more. What generally goes under the name of spirituality is merely the record of past methods."

De Mello sums this up: "Don't cut the person to fit the coat."[1] I concluded that this was what I was attempting to do when following others' methods for meditation.

*Don't cut the person to fit the coat.*
—Anthony de Mello

Some contemporary teachers, such as John O'Donohue, do not encourage any methods of meditation, knowing that the human mind can write any method in stone and go about telling the world that it is the one true way. When the landscape of the psyche shifts, the methods that we use may no longer work in service of inner transformation.

In reality, meditation can happen in many ways. Prominent teacher and author Ram Dass tells a story about a woman who sat in the front row and knitted through his whole lecture on sitting meditation. Afterward she came up to him and said, "I have the same experiences you described through my knitting."

Any activity that allows the mind to slow down and become quiet can be considered meditation. A meditative state occurs when we step out of ordinary clock time into dreamtime. We feel at peace and fully present to the activity. By this definition, meditation could be as varied as writing a book or playing

*Absolutely unmixed attention is prayer.*
—Simone Weil

a sophisticated computer game. The qualities of flow and focus are central and the activity must remain relatively free of compulsive behavior. Then these experiences have the potential to be fruitful meditation.

My lack of success with sitting meditation motivated me to find a more effective way to handle my chaotic mind. Walking—moving my body—drains off a great deal of excess energy. I can begin to slow down my thought process, become conscious of my breath, and allow my awareness to rest in my body. This is a key for many of us "failed meditators."

## A Practice as Compared to a Discipline

Walking the labyrinth is a practice, not necessarily a discipline. A practice is more flexible than a discipline. A discipline is usually done at a certain time each day. There are specific methods or techniques to enter into it. The practice of labyrinth walking is guided by what you need from the walk. I encourage people to walk the labyrinth when they feel drawn to do so. It may be a bonding activity to do when friends visit, a way to focus your thoughts before a therapy session, or a ritual container to say your prayers before you return to your oncologist hoping for test results clear of cancer.

Use the labyrinth when it calls you. When you want the benefits of a quiet mind, a prayerful heart, a release from controlling behavior, find your way to a labyrinth. Some people use it weekly, others casually, others intensely for a period of time to prepare for a specific event such as surgery or to recover from a trauma. Find your own rhythm with it, but don't be so loose with it that it slips out of your life. Remember, inner transformation, says the Master, is the purpose of the spiritual life.

Discipline and practice are not opposed to each other. Meditators who have a regular discipline of sitting meditation relate to the labyrinth very well. In fact, the discipline that their practice teaches helps quiet their mind throughout the walk, whereas others who have not developed these skills may struggle with this in the beginning. Discipline and practice truly go hand in hand, but for those who shy away from even the thought of a discipline, the term "practice" is more user-friendly, more accessible, and not fraught with dos and don'ts that can add to the distractions of a busy, unruly mind.

One of the cornerstone teachings of walking the labyrinth is that there is no right way or wrong way to use it. This is important because the labyrinth can be usurped into being a rigid system of rules. By understanding that there's no right way or wrong way to walk a labyrinth, the responsibility is on you to determine what you need and how you want to use it. You must claim your own inner authority and tailor the walk to your needs if you are to use it effectively. Then you will be developing your own practice, not following someone else's. You will not have to "cut the person to fit the coat."

## The Grail Castle: The World in between Worlds

The Grail Castle is a central symbol in the Grail stories. It holds the Grail, but it is very hard to find. It does not exist on the physical earth, but rather in that mysterious place in between the worlds. This is the imaginal realm, which can be experienced, but not seen with the human eye. It is a zone that we walk in and out of from time to time, but we cannot force our way into it. It is the place where we meet our muse, the portal to the symbolic world. In it rests the fountain of creative flow that we draw upon during a transformative act. It is the source where the images for a painting that speaks to the universal soul comes from. It is the metaphoric world that allows us to release self-hatred that rots our inner beings.

The labyrinth is a physical portal to this unseen world of flow. For this reason, the labyrinth is a watering hole for the spirit, inviting us to drink. The process in this book, and specifically this section, is to guide you through this portal, so you may use this astounding tool to further your inner transformation; to heal and transform.

## The Use of Questions

Surprisingly, very early on in his search, Parzival finds the Grail Castle where he is a guest of honor at a fantastic banquet. However, Parzival is unable to be present in the moment with a compassionate heart. When the injured king is brought into the room on a stretcher to enjoy the feast as best he can, Parzival fails to ask the question: Dear King, what ails thee? His heart is unavailable to hear the woeful story of the king. Parzival must ask this question to bring the Grail King's suffering into the realm of consciousness. This would heal the king and bring life back to his parched and barren kingdom.

The Swiss psychiatrist Carl Jung makes the point that the world is in continual transformation. The eternal rhythm of the human psyche as well as the natural world is to build up and pull down, to integrate and disintegrate. To reap the harvest of this process we must step into it and interrupt it. He illustrates this point using the example of an apple tree. It blossoms in the spring and produces apples in the early fall; these will drop to the ground and decay into the soil by winter unless the farmer gathers up the apples. The act of gathering the apples interrupts the eternal system of growth and decay, expansion and contraction. Just like the farmer, we change the course of this process by bringing consciousness to it. The way to do this is through questions and inquiries that will bring symbols from the unconscious processes into conscious awareness.[2]

We must learn the tough lesson Parzival had to learn: it is wise to ask the questions stirred by what life presents to us. To be able to ask an insightful question is a worthy trait. The questions change depending upon our circumstances and our maturity, but using questions is a way of staying awake and present to the unconscious dynamics from which our lives manifest.

A second reason for questions: If we do not know what we seek, we are less likely to find it. If we are without goals and cannot focus on the tasks that lead to accomplishing it, we are rudderless in an ocean of choice. The questions I hear from the people I meet around the labyrinth are questions about guiding a healing process, about truly "walking our talk," and about the mystery of life. In the next chapter, "Four Guidelines to Gauge Your Spiritual Growth," we will begin to answer the question: What are our lives like when we mature spiritually?

# One

# Four Guidelines
# to Gauge Your
# Spiritual Growth

*When we meet real tragedy in life, we can react in two ways—either by losing hope and falling into self-destructive habits, or by using the challenge to find our inner strength.*

—The Dalai Lama

There are many definitions of spirituality. I prefer not to use the ones that come from academia; they are often too hard to understand and have little practical application. We seekers aren't looking for dry definitions; we're seeking methods and teachings that will help Spirit permeate every moment of our lives. We want to be better people.

Over the years four qualities have woven their way into my work. I offer them as guidelines for your work with the labyrinth. If you are on a spiritual path—any path from the rich traditions of the world's religions—to live a healed and transformed life, you want to:

*If we attempt to act and do things for others or for the world without deepening our own self-understanding, our own freedom, integrity and capacity to love, we will not have anything to give to others. We will communicate nothing but the contagion of our own obsessions, our aggressiveness, our own ego-centered ambitions.* —Thomas Merton

- Deepen your compassion
- Lessen your judgments
- Increase your patience
- Find your purpose and share it with the world

These four guidelines are ideals; you may never develop all of them fully, but they point in the direction you want to go. If you reflect upon your life over the last year, you can begin to answer the questions:

- Have I deepened my compassion for my family, my friends, and the strangers who cross my path?
- Have I lessened my judgments about my loved ones and those I meet?
- Have I increased my patience with my loved ones and those I meet on the path?
- Have I found my purpose, and nurtured it, so I can be of service to the world?

What stops these qualities from becoming a deeper part of your life? There is no judgment in these questions; they offer a way to reflect upon your spiritual growth.

*(Feminine) wisdom is rooted in experience, in compassion. She thinks with her heart and is more concerned with the processes than with the products of a life lived fully. She does not value the presence of power but the power of presence.*

—Jill Mellick

# To Deepen in Compassion

The *American Heritage Dictionary* defines compassion as the "deep feeling of sharing the suffering of another in the inclination to give aid or support." A second definition is "mercy."

Compassion is a basic quality that all religious traditions strive to cultivate within their followers. However, in our technologically sophisticated world, we see catastrophes weekly, if not daily in news reports. There is an earthquake in Iran, a car bomb in Israel, or a hurricane in New Orleans; a tsunami in southern Asia, people dying of AIDS in Africa, or a famine in Sudan. Some catastrophes we ignore, others we pay attention to and send money, clothes, and medical supplies. What is it that makes us turn our faces away? What is it that opens our hearts?

Compassion is very close to sympathy, when you feel connected to another's suffering. But it is not pity, which is when you feel sorry for someone. Compassion is empathy; a feeling, a sensing—perhaps a knowing—what another person is going through even though you are not experiencing the suffering directly. Compassion does not always carry the impulse to step in and lend a helping hand. But it always carries its own healing force. Usually when someone feels compassion emanating from another person, both are aware of it in that moment. Compassion is developed as you break through the "glass bottles of your egos"[1] into the world of the heart.

Deepening our compassion is one of the great spiritual challenges of our times. Compassion develops through life experiences and is tempered by our own suffering. Life can harden your heart. You can have experiences that leave you hurt and demoralized but compassion develops as you experience the pain contained within the difficult situations in your own life. Once you suffer, you are more sensitive to the suffering of others. Once you experience suffering, and if it has brought you to your knees, you do not wish it upon anyone else.

If you can feel compassion, you are more forgiving and you become more flexible. It permits more room for gentleness; a softness can come through even if you have to be firm in your dealings with others. To stand in compassion is to see the world through soft eyes. The mind is quiet and the heart is receptive. Suggestions as to how to reach a soft-eyed state are offered in chapter 7, "Shadow Work."

## To Lessen Your Judgments

To lessen your judgments against yourself and others is a significant spiritual practice. Judgment differs from assessment or evaluation. Of course you need to use your judgment as you move through your day. You need to assess whether your sixteen-year-old neighbor will be a responsible babysitter. You need to use your judgment to choose good-hearted people for your organization, the people you work with, and as friends.

The kind of judgment that can get in your way is based on prejudices, which usually means it is based on very little information. I remember meeting Archbishop Desmond Tutu when he visited General Theological Seminary in New York City in the early 1980s. Someone asked him what the most painful thing he ever experienced in his life was. He responded **If you judge someone, you will never** quickly: "Being judged by the color of my **learn about the person.** skin instead of who I truly am."

If you judge someone, you will never learn about the person. You will never learn who they are. You will only confirm your set opinions. Early one morning I was in Grace Cathedral soon after the tapestry labyrinth had been placed there. A distraught woman came up to me and demanded that I remove a young woman from the labyrinth. I looked over to see a young woman dressed in a modern corporate outfit apparently on her way to work after her walk. The woman who complained to me was upset that the young woman was wearing a pinstriped suit that had shorts instead of a longer skirt. She was dressed appropriately for her age and for the style of the day, but this woman did not see that. She could not reflect upon why she was so upset or demanding of me to carry out her wishes. What was sad was that she was neither embarrassed by her behavior nor remotely aware of what prompted her strong reaction. Her judgment had been triggered unconsciously.

I do not recall what I said to her. She became very unhappy with me when I did not respond to her demand and she walked off in a huff. The young woman completed her labyrinth walk and left the cathedral unaware of these events. We can all have episodes like this in our lives. Judgments can remain invisible to us. They can be so automatic and so impenetrable to reflection that we never realize how they severely limit our worldview. Our task is to lessen our judgments and to embrace the possibilities of learning from others. There will be exercises on working with judgment in the "Shadow Work" and "Healing" chapters.

# To Increase Patience

We all admire patient people. Patience is a wonderful quality and we feel cared for when someone is patient with us. To increase patience within our beings is an important part of a spiritual practice.

 *Patience begets patience.* —St. Francis

In my struggle to increase my patience with myself and those around me, I find myself agreeing with St. Francis: the more patient you are in one setting, the easier it is to be in another. Patience builds upon patience. It is like developing a muscle. The more you use it, the stronger it gets.

Impatience is a reaction. Patience is a response. There needs to be within you a place to go to find that response, rather than just "flying off the handle." Most forms of meditation help to develop this muscle. They help you to find that spaciousness inside that is not at the mercy of what happens around you. When you have a spacious sense within, you are connected to that inner chamber where you can go and rest and, if need be, wait.

Waiting is hard for just about everyone. The world is hyperactive, full of noise, speed, and activity. People are somehow deemed less important if they are not busy or in a hurry. The wisdom of slowing down is often overlooked. We will revisit the experience of waiting in chapter 8, "Soul Assignment."

Buddhist teacher and monk Thich Nhat Hanh teaches "Red Light Meditation," where he encourages us to use each red light we encounter while driving as a moment of meditation. Instead of feeling impatience, welcome these moments as a "time-out" to breathe and reflect. He suggests doing the same when the phone rings—use the sound of the ring as an invitation into awareness, just like a meditation bell. Become awake to your circumstances as you slowly move to answer the phone. Such moments can give us back to ourselves. And, of course, we can always let the answering machine pick up the call.

## To Find Your Purpose and Share It with the World

One quote that has resonated with many people over the years is from Søren Kierkegaard: "Every human being comes to earth with sealed orders." It strikes a chord in people because so many of us have the intuitive feeling that there is some special assignment that we have to fulfill. This is why we were born.

 *Every human being comes to earth with sealed orders.* —Søren Kierkegaard

Psychologist and author Jean Houston calls this Divine Entelechy; James Hillman, the founder of *Analytical Psychology*, refers to it as the acorn theory. Like the acorn that contains the mighty oak, everything within you is encoded in a certain way for you to blossom to your fullest. The spiritual task is to develop your potential to the fullest. Not everyone is able to do this. Obstacles are challenges to your inventiveness and tenacity. Hurdles get put in your way that will slow you down and frustrate you. But if you have a practice that supports your efforts, you can reach into your depths and find the strength.

Not every purpose is a direct service to the world. Many have indirect benefits to the broader community. For instance, you may have had a passion for antique trains all your life. You collected them, shared them at

Christmas with your family, and in your last years gave them to your grandchildren. Is this of service to the world? Indirectly, I think it is. The impact of your having found your passion can provide inspiration for others. The memory of you working with the trains will find a home in your children's and grandchildren's hearts.

Other things you do may have a direct impact. Every time I travel I am thankful to the person who put wheels on suitcases. Is this a service to the world? Certainly.

You can get bogged down in finding your purpose if you feel you have to do something big with significant impact. I am reminded of what twelfth-century mystic Hildegard of Bingen wrote—that your gift does not have to be unique, but it needs to be original. You don't need to find something that is one of a kind. What you want to find and offer is something authentic to who you are. Whatever you offer, it should come from your own sense of self, which generates originality.

I am amazed by the number of people who begin to find their life's purpose and shape their life's work through walking the labyrinth. It is certainly true for me, and I have seen many others whose gifts are opened, whether it be teaching, organizing, writing, or speaking. It is as though the labyrinth "births" people into their gifts. This does not happen without taking risks, of course, but the unfolding of people's lives is quite dramatic when this powerful archetypal energy is activated. You are freed to take courageous action on your own behalf. We will continue this topic in chapter 8, "Soul Assignment."

 *Your gift does not have to be unique, but it needs to be original.* —Hildegard of Bingen

# Two

# LESSONS OF THE
# LABYRINTH

*Walking the labyrinth clears the mind and gives insight into the spiritual jour-
ney. It urges action. It calms people in the throes of life transitions. It helps
them see their lives in the context of a path, a pilgrimage. They realize that
they are not human beings on a spiritual path, but spiritual beings on a human path.*

—From *Walking a Sacred Path*

The labyrinth is a great teacher. It offers strong and clear boundaries that allow you to feel safe inside. It has a clear beginning,
middle, and end, so you have the sense of a spiritual exercise as
well as a ritual activity that you can share with others.

Within the labyrinth, your interior world can become clear to you. You
can see through the otherwise obscured thoughts and blocked feelings. An
apt comparison is snorkeling in the Caribbean. As soon as you gear up and
go underwater, a new world opens to you. The noise of the world becomes
muffled and remote. Time melts into your experience and seems to disappear. In these moments you become aware of color, light, and the beauty

of the underwater world. This can happen in the labyrinth as well. Time can disappear and the busy world around you becomes a muffled backdrop. In this world we can experience emotions, images, and memories within us we never paid attention to before.

As an example: Once when I was walking the labyrinth in Chartres, I was feeling stuck in my work; it felt as if there was no movement. As I walked, the first image that came to me was that I was forced up against a ceiling with no way to break through. Then I took the sensation of being pressed against something from the image and let myself intensify it in my body. Through this, I became aware that I was holding back in my body. My muscles were taut and rigid as if bracing for an impact. As I walked, I concentrated on letting these muscles relax, but in order to do that, I had to acknowledge the fear that they were holding. It was the fear of moving ahead, of taking the next step in my professional life.

The labyrinth is an archetypal pattern. The circle is a universal form, found in every culture in the world. It communicates unity and wholeness. Contained within this circle is a complex spiral that, as you walk it, takes you deeper into your center. The literal becomes figurative, and the figurative becomes literal. The literal path of the labyrinth—whether it be paint applied to canvas, terrazzo stone inlaid in a wood floor, or rocks laid out on dirt—becomes the Path of Life. Over time, you can develop a deep relationship with the labyrinth. It becomes a trustworthy friend. For those of us who have been betrayed and mistrust people, the fact that it is a physical symbol, not a living person, is a comforting feature as well.

As Keith Critchlow, professor of Islamic Studies at the Royal Academy in London, says, "Not only are the exact cosmic rhythms built into it, but as well, the other sacred measures that represent our relationship to the 'journey back' to our spiritual wholeness."[1] The structure, the rhythm of the walk, and the bodily movement of walking in a complex spiral pattern offer us spiritual and psychological benefits that I want to discuss in this chapter.

## Quieting the Mind

The mind can quiet in any number of ways. I have friends who love to needlepoint. Others paint just for the pleasure of it. A quiet mind is pleasurable and refreshing: when we are at peace we often lose track of time and feel calm for hours on end.

The labyrinth channels the anxious and chaotic energy that is at the core of the mental "static" you experience when you

*To the quiet mind, the world surrenders.*
—Huston Smith

attempt to quiet the mind. When stress increases, so does the chaotic mental energy that makes it so hard to sustain concentration.

In scientific studies of meditation, two approaches have been identified that handle this static. The first is concentration. The objective of the concentration methods is to dis-identify with your thoughts. Thoughts can be slowed down, but never truly stopped. But nurturing a practice gives us a choice over what to do with these thoughts. Thought can be like a flowing river moving throughout your mind, which can be a pleasurable experience. If we grab on to one thought, however, we then are attached to it. Learning to detach from thought brings us into the refreshing realm of interior silence.

Repeated phrases or sacred words—mantras—help focus concentration. The mind does not stop thinking altogether, but it can be slowed and focused. The thinking mind can be like a large undisciplined dog or a stubborn, angry donkey. It has its own ways of doing things and we don't realize this until we attempt to tame it. A neutral or positive phrase repeated in your mind is like giving the dog a bone to chew on. You contain and focus your energy. Likewise, when thoughts come into your mind, if you return to your repeated phrase you can refocus your concentration. The labyrinth is an excellent place to practice concentration methods. During the first stage of the walk I may use a repeated phrase, and in the center, let go of the phrase, dropping it into a deep silence.

A second way to quiet the mind is through awareness. These methods invite you to pay attention to your thoughts. Not the chattering mind, but the deeper thoughts that flow through you. If you had a printed ticker tape of all that goes through your mind during one day, it would be miles long! Upon reading the printout of these thoughts, you'd find one or two thoughts consistently repeated. Perhaps a long-held hurt is not resolved. Or you want a raise and you rehearse how to ask for it. The mind can be stuck on these things and if the mind is stuck, you are too.

**What's the difference between a fifty-year-old immature person and a fifty-year-old mature person? The ability to learn from their experiences.**

Awareness methods include visualization, active imagination, and focusing techniques. In part 2, I offer ways to use the labyrinth for healing, such as asking for forgiveness, looking at repeated patterns (in "Shadow Work"), and clarifying your passion in life. Most of these suggestions are awareness methods.

# Self-Reflection

The labyrinth nurtures the capacity to reflect. In reflection you review your behavior and the choices you are making or have made. To reflect upon your experiences is the only way you learn the art of being human.

Self-reflection is always a nonjudgmental process. If you are judging yourself, that becomes the focus of your reflection. Most often we are afraid to look within because we are afraid of what we will find there. If we are unhappy with who we are or blame ourselves for an incident that occurred in the past, we fear that our reflection will arouse all the negative voices within us. To allow self-reflection we have to come to terms with our inner critical voices. (See chapter 6, "Healing.")

Cultivating self-reflection is one of the greatest gifts you can give to yourself and the ones you love. We all know people who cannot reflect. They blame their behavior on others because they cannot ask the simple question, "What is my role in this situation?" They go through life unaware of their impact on others. Or, quietly they are at war within, guarding against unwanted thoughts that are attempting to yield insight. Coming to peace within ourselves and with those we love is a spiritual task. It begins with self-acceptance.

**Cultivating self-reflection is one of the greatest gifts you can give to yourself and the ones you love.**

## Spaciousness Allows Responsiveness

When a spiritual practice begins to work, you develop a sense of spaciousness within, a quiet, calm place. A gentle, wise voice of guidance begins to take root that allows you to choose the best ways to respond to life's challenges.

Earlier, I touched upon the difference between being reactive and responsive in the context of impatience and patience. That is a small example of what I am referring to here. Reactivity is replaced with thoughtfulness. If you experience a flash of anger, you can use the "space" inside to reflect on it before responding.

The practice of walking the labyrinth allows you to engender this spacious feeling internally. Spaciousness within allows you to have a repertoire of responses from which to choose. When your practice is working for you, there is more choice over your thoughts and actions, and you'll be better able to channel your feelings in constructive ways. (See "Set an Intention" in chapter 4 for a specific exercise to use when facing a life situation you fear you may handle poorly.)

## Enlivening the Body

The wants and needs of the body are either indulged far too much in Western culture, or ignored altogether. Both of these extremes result in addictive behaviors and a confused relationship to our bodies. In the labyrinth, our bodies often speak up. We can become aware of physical issues we may have been oblivious to.

Some people report that while walking the labyrinth, they feel relief from chronic pain and stiffness. Though there is no hard scientific research to understand this phenomenon, I am always glad when labyrinth walking produces this result.

Others may experience sharp pains, dull aches, muscle contractions, and other kinds of messages from the body that never occur outside the labyrinth. These can be explored during the labyrinth walk. For example, one woman came up to me after two consecutive walks in the labyrinth. She described the first as joyous and uplifting. During the second walk, she had a fleeting memory of a deceased sibling and then experienced a sharp pain in her intestines. This scared her and she walked off the labyrinth, leaving the pain unexplored. We will expand this concept and see how she could have worked with this in the "Reconnecting with Your Body" section of chapter 6.

*There is a vitality, a life force, a quickening that is translated through you into action, and because there is only one you in all time, this expression is unique. . . . You have to keep open and aware directly to the urges that motivate you. Keep the channel open.* —Martha Graham

## Mind/Body/Spirit Integration

Teaching the labyrinth is like teaching fish to swim. It is easy and natural for most people to enter into a different realm of consciousness. Soon after you enter the labyrinth, the challenge of following the highly structured pattern takes over and you lose any remaining self-consciousness.

The labyrinth predates Descartes' worldview that embraced a split between the body, mind, and Spirit. Walking it literally opens a new realm. This world has been lost for many people so it may seem strange at first, which is why I am writing this book. In the labyrinth, a whole, integrated world presents itself. You can have a heart-to-heart talk with your body. You can have a heart-to-heart talk with Spirit. They all flow together in the labyrinth.

This is not always a comfortable state to be in, especially for those who are afraid that they will lose control. Usually we do not attempt to explore the divisions between mind, body, and Spirit unless we are sick or injured or we can't experience bodily pleasure. These challenges can take us deeper into ourselves. We may have stored experiences of physical or emotional abuse that need to be released. The labyrinth is a unique avenue that has helped thousands of people find a deeper integration within. This newly found state releases new energies so we can live our lives more fully.

*If we look at the world traditions at their best, we discover a distillation of wisdom of the human race.* —Huston Smith

## We Are All on the Path Together

When we walk the labyrinth with others, we get a sense that we are not going through life alone. We are all on the Path together. We are united by the fact that we all live in the human body. We all come into life the same way and we must all shed this mortal coil at some unknown point in time. We all live on the same planet—a fragile island home—during unique and challenging times. Though Western culture has nurtured the illusion that humans are in charge, we are at the mercy of forces of nature as well as our own ignorance in handling our resources so our life on this planet has become threatened.

A few people have a difficult time when walking with twenty or more people. They feel distracted from their meditation. I discuss this further in "The Art of Labyrinth Walking."

## EVERYONE'S JOURNEY TO THE DIVINE IS UNIQUE

At the beginning of a workshop for beginners I was leading, one woman spoke with strong feelings. She said that the single path of the labyrinth was not a good metaphor for the spiritual journey. It did not capture that there are many ways to the Divine. Since she had not walked a labyrinth yet, I encouraged her to experience it and we would take up her point in the afternoon reflection session. At the close of the workshop, we gathered to share our reflections and I returned to her statement. She immediately said, "Never mind. I got it."

Since the body/mind/Spirit is unified in the labyrinth, many paradoxes appear. "The one is many and the many are one" is a teaching that you can bodily experience in the labyrinth. A second paradox is that we are alone together. What this woman understood was the paradox that we are all on the Path together, yet walking it in our own unique ways.

Quite often, as you connect to the deep intuitive level within yourself, nurtured by the practice of labyrinth walking, you embrace what is unfolding as sacred. An experience of the sacred is unique to each of us. There are commonalities, but each of us has and holds our own experiences. No one can argue with these experiences, because they are ours alone. Everyone has to do this journey on their own, though it is helpful to have an experienced person in your life who can guide you on the journey.

## Walking in Groups: Make Room for One Another

Although often just one or two people may be walking a labyrinth at one time, my work usually has a group focus. Depending upon the size of the labyrinth, thirty to forty-five people may be walking it together. Walking the labyrinth is an enriching group experience. People quickly realize that they are sharing common space and that you cannot just elbow your way to the center. There is a literal lesson in that we have to make space for one another.

My friend François Legaux, dean emeritus of Chartres Cathedral and honorary canon of Grace Cathedral, describes labyrinth walking as "a lesson in tolerance." Indeed it can be, especially if someone is walking backwards or very slowly, is disrespectful of your space, or is having a powerful release of tears that you find difficult to be receptive to.

Walking the labyrinth challenges our assumption that a meditation is done alone—usually with eyes closed—and does not include others. The precious sense of "it's just God and me" is taken away. Walking the labyrinth with others is interactive. You may rub elbows with another person. Or you may reach out to hug a dear friend.

> *Now, in a century with eyes wide open to the evils of domination, the sin of exclusiveness, the other humanity of the feminine, a God of infinitely gentle heart waits for all of us outside of old systems and old rules at someplace new.*
>
> —Joan Chittister

Labyrinth walking opens people up to another possibility: we are literally all sharing the space in whatever size labyrinth we are walking. We realize that we are sharing the planet and its limited (and diminishing) natural resources. It is a sobering thought that we truly need to learn to share our space and our resources.

# The Feminine Archetype: Receptivity and Flow

Once you find your own natural pace, you can acclimate yourself to the rhythm of others. Your walking begins to flow with those around you. The highly structured pattern of various 180-degree turns—from tight ones to more spacious ones—provides a rhythm that the psyche needs in order to calm down and open up.

Being in an intuitive flow is one of the most refreshing activities we can do. Images burst forth: unwinding, uncoiling, participating in the cosmic dance. This flow is renewing and opens our creative channels. Being able to open the doors to our intuitive world is of great value. "The Labyrinth is a perfect symbol of the dance between Soul and Spirit,"[2] says Jungian analyst Sylvia Senensky. And when the soul and the Spirit dance together on the physical plane, new capacities emerge, new ways of imagining the world appear. Whatever you choose to call it—the feminine face of God, the receptive archetype, the feminine archetype—it gives us another way of walking the Path of Life: softly, with a compassionate heart and an open mind. We learn to walk soft-eyed with a quiet, nonjudgmental perspective. We learn to walk respectfully with others, celebrating our differences. All the world's religious traditions in their most profound forms teach these concepts. The labyrinth allows us to experience them.

The lessons of the labyrinth can be profound. To reap the benefits of walking the labyrinth, it is helpful to know the basics of walking. "The Art of Labyrinth Walking" and "Applications" follow this chapter.

# Three

# THE ART OF
# LABYRINTH WALKING

*Teaching people to walk the labyrinth is like teaching fish to swim.*

A brief orientation to the labyrinth helps beginners by answering questions such as How do I walk the labyrinth? and What am I to gain from the experience? Once these questions are addressed, however briefly, the cognitive mind seems to accept the exercise. Otherwise, if the thinking mind is uncomfortable it creates distraction through excessive thought. All the following teachings make up the art of labyrinth walking.

## Labyrinth Terminology

Start by becoming familiar with the terminology:

**Circuits:** The number of times the path goes around the center. Since the labyrinth is not a maze, we cannot use the term "paths" in the plural. There is only one path.

**Center:** The center of the labyrinth is an important symbol. In meditative walking, the center is never described as the goal; this rings of achievement—ego-oriented activity that is counter to the spiritual path. In the tradition of pilgrimage, the center of the Chartres labyrinth is called the New Jerusalem.

**The petals:** The Chartres-style labyrinth has six petals around the center. They offer many layers of symbols, including the six days of Creation, and the rose and the lily symbolic of Mary and of rebirth. Six is also the symbol for Aphrodite. The petals are unique to the Chartres labyrinth. Each petal has a name. (See "Use the Six-Petal Meditation" in "Applications.")

**Labrys:** The double-ax, or butterfly, pattern between the turns on the path are called labrys. The Medieval Eleven-Circuit Labyrinth has ten labrys that form a cruciform.

**Lunations:** The outer cusps and foils that encircle the Chartres-style Medieval Eleven-Circuit Labyrinth are called lunations. There are twenty-eight per quadrant and they are symbolic of the lunar cycle. These are unique to this labyrinth.

**Left-handed or right-handed labyrinth:** The first turn determines whether it is a left-handed or right-handed labyrinth. In a left-handed labyrinth, the first turn goes to the left. In a right-handed labyrinth, the first turn goes to the right. The Medieval Eleven-Circuit Labyrinth is always a left-handed labyrinth. The Classical Seven-Circuit Labyrinth can be either left- or right-handed.

**Field:** The space between the borders of the path. Some people call this the "wall," though this creates the wrong impression unless, as in some labyrinths, there is a literal wall of turf, stone, or some other material between the circuits.

**Linear labyrinth:** In this style of labyrinth, such as from the Roman tradition, the path moves in a predictable pattern from one quadrant to the next until you reach the center. You always know where you are in a linear labyrinth.

**Nonlinear labyrinth:** In a nonlinear labyrinth, such as the Medieval Eleven-Circuit Labyrinth, the path moves through the four quadrants in a nonsequential way. This creates a feeling of being lost and challenges the mind to focus more intensely.

## Common Questions

*What is a labyrinth?*
A labyrinth is a pattern, usually in the form of a large circle, that has one path, beginning at the outer edge and leading in a circuitous way into the center. Labyrinths found in medieval churches and cathedrals are flat to the floor and called pavement or church labyrinths. They can also be made out of hedges, earthen mounds, or other materials that give them dimension.

Some labyrinths offer a choice to go either right or left a few paces in from the entry. But once you make the choice, you follow a consistent, reliable path that will lead you to the center. This may vary with contemporary labyrinths.

*What is the difference between a labyrinth and a maze?*
Mazes and labyrinths have been confused with one another for centuries. In French, there is only one word for both: labyrinth. Technically, a labyrinth is unicursal, having one path, and a maze is multicursal, having many paths. However, definitions like this perpetuate the confusion. A labyrinth has no dead ends, cul-de-sacs, or multiple entrances and has one clear (if circuitous) path to the center. A maze is a game, a cognitive challenge to see how quickly one can find the way to the goal. There is an easy way to make the distinction: a maze is designed to make you lose your way and a labyrinth is designed to help you find your way.

**A maze is designed to make you lose your way and a labyrinth is designed to help you find your way.**

*What is an archetypal labyrinth?*
Archetypal labyrinths are ones that have been created anonymously, perfected over time, and passed down through the ages to new generations. They have been developed collectively through the teachings of a sacred tradition, mostly unknown to us today. They reliably transform human consciousness. They are in the public domain.

*How does an archetypal labyrinth differ from a contemporary one?*
Contemporary labyrinths are ones made by modern enthusiasts. They are fun to make and often build a sense of community as well, but most likely

will not carry the transforming power of the Classical Seven-Circuit, the Medieval Eleven-Circuit, or other archetypal patterns. The most effective contemporary labyrinths are the ones that extend a metaphor meaningful to the person walking it. Many contemporary labyrinths are copyrighted.

*How do I know if a labyrinth walk is effective?*
Your experience is your guide. Find your pace and your mind should become peaceful or flowing, though this may not happen on the first walk if your mind is unruly or fending off difficult thoughts. When the mind is quiet, a stream of thoughts, memories, dream fragments, insights, and images comes into awareness. This is stirred by the act of walking, as well as by the structure of the labyrinth. Each labyrinth walk is different even if it is on the same labyrinth. This is true for the archetypal Medieval Eleven-Circuit Labyrinth and the Seven-Circuit as well. Its placement, the intent of the people making it, the materials, the tenor of the land, the season, what you are grappling with—all these factors affect the impact of the labyrinth walk, even if you walk the same labyrinth every day. Experience your experience and you will get a sense of its impact on you. Remember, the impact may come quite a while after the walk: a prayer may be answered or a resolution to a question revealed. A journaling process is helpful to capture these experiences.

*What happens if I get lost?*
The labyrinth is not designed to have you get lost. However, since the path is narrow and you may be moving around others or meeting them on the return (also called reflection) path, you can lose your concentration. If you get lost going into the labyrinth, you wind up back at the entrance not

having reached the center. If you get lost on your way out, you wind up back in the center. This can be an upsetting experience, but keep in mind that this is not a high-risk activity. Perfectionists may berate themselves for making a mistake. Those who are fearful of failure may have their fear mirrored back to them. Use everything that happens to you in the labyrinth as a metaphor. Ask yourself: What can I learn from this experience?

### What if nothing happens?

Something always happens in the labyrinth. Thoughts and feelings that you may be in the habit of dismissing—rather than recognizing—may attempt to come into awareness. If you push them back into unconsciousness, the experience is of confused, fleeting thoughts and feelings. Expectations can also be at work. An expectation to have something else happen other than what occurs in the labyrinth leads to a sense of emptiness. Experience your experience.

### Why were labyrinths destroyed?

As the Western world embraced the scientific, empirical paradigm, labyrinths fell into disuse. If you cannot see it, count it, or measure it, it must not be worth paying attention to was the thinking, so these great intuitive blueprints became devalued in the Western world. Unfortunately, because the Christian church at that time attempted to fit in with the scientific paradigm, labyrinths became an embarrassment to the church. These attitudes still linger today.

### Is the labyrinth sacred?

"Sacred" means different things to different people. If you define sacred as where the veil is thin, where the invisible world touches the visible, then yes, the labyrinth is sacred.

What is sacred to one person may not be to another. Many tourists can walk into Grace or Chartres Cathedral and never be touched by the beauty and awe of the labyrinth. Others will spend time to pray, reflect, and walk the labyrinth. Sacredness, like beauty, is in the eye of the beholder.

### Can children use the labyrinth?

Children love the labyrinth. They can run it, skip it, and "wind" their way into the center. It often brings out the spiritual nature in children.

It is best if a number of children walk the labyrinth together. If the leader does not implement some sort of structure, it can be bedlam, but the children will have fun. Children should be supervised if they are walking with adults who are there to meditate.

The game of hopscotch is thought to be derived from the labyrinth. Stand on the outside edge of the labyrinth at any of the three directions that are not the entrance. If you enter at one of these sides and step on the turns, with the labrys between your feet, you will discover a one-two-one-two pattern.

> *"It had never occurred to me that a labyrinth would be so attractive to children until I watched Daniel and Rebekah trace it and walk the labyrinth. There was something in the experience that touched their spirituality."* —A workshop participant

### Why is the path narrow in the labyrinth?

Most labyrinths have a narrow path because this focuses the attention of the walker more easily. It takes a certain level of concentration to walk the labyrinth, which is why labyrinths are effective with children and adults struggling with attention deficit disorder.

There are labyrinths with wide paths, but their use is slightly different—they can build community, beautify a park, serve as an exercise for the elderly, or provide a place for meditation for people in wheelchairs.

## Meditative Walking

There are two ways to walk a labyrinth: as a walking meditation or as part of a ceremony, exercise, or ritual. I will talk about meditative walking in this section because it includes all the basic teaching concerning how to walk a labyrinth. Ritual and ceremonial use—including the processional method—will be in chapter 9, "Initiatory Rituals."

Usually I teach the use of the labyrinth as a walking meditation since there is a pressing need to quiet our minds and to find an effective way to meditate. In this area the labyrinth is truly a gift. Over the years I've learned that it is best to introduce first-time walkers to meditative walking rather than ritual use. Once I presented a labyrinth workshop at a church in Southern California. As I began to explain the labyrinth, I could feel that there was confusion in the group. I asked if people had used a labyrinth before and discovered that another person had done an earlier workshop but had used a problem-solving method (placing a question on each turn) for their first walk. The participants were confused by what I was telling them: they had no idea that the labyrinth could be used for meditation. This group hadn't grasped the labyrinth's full potential.

*I was once spiritually ill—we all pass through that—but one day the intelligence of my soul cured me.*
                                        —Meister Eckhart

# The Three Rs

Over the years the language used to describe the stages of the walking meditation has evolved to reflect a new understanding. In the early years it was important to keep the language describing the process behind the labyrinth in tune with the well-educated congregation of Grace Cathedral, so I referred to the walk as having three stages: purgation, illumination, and union (Theresa of Avila's description of the journey to God called the Three Fold Path originally from Proctus and Plotinus). However, as the labyrinth became more accepted, there was less need to use this specific terminology to ground the walking meditation practice in tradition. The three stages became the three Rs—releasing, receiving, and returning and these descriptors have been useful for many years, especially in secular settings.

# The Four Rs

Recently, Veriditas hosted theologian and spokesperson for Creation Spirituality Matthew Fox at Chartres Cathedral for our annual Walking a Sacred Path program. We agreed that we wanted our work to be more in alignment. Though I referred in my first book to the Four Fold Path—which is looked at with suspicion because it embraces original blessing instead of Augustine's concept of original sin—I did not emphasize it.

Now it is time, so I offer a way to incorporate the fact that we are born blessed and not held prisoner to teachings that ingrain in humans that we were born in original sin. So, I offer the Four Rs.

The Four Fold Path incorporates the transformational, yet forgotten, teachings, the core of which is from the Wisdom literature in the Hebrew Scriptures. They are the Via Positiva (blessing), the Via Negativa (emptying), the Via Creativa (receiving the creative spirit), and Via Transformativa (the transformed person transforms the community.)[1]

The first stage is *remembering*. (Via Positiva) As you are gathering your thoughts, preparing to begin your walk, remember you are blessed. All that we have, all that we are is a blessing from the Divine. Often in my work with groups, there is a line at the labyrinth as people wait to walk; this is the time to literally count your blessings.

The second stage is *releasing* (Via Negativa) or letting go, quieting, opening, emptying, or shedding. This stage begins at the entrance and ends at the center.

In the center is *receiving* (Via Creativa). Having emptied, there is spaciousness within to receive the creative spirit. Receiving guidance, interior silence, a creative idea, and a sense of peace are only a few experiences that can occur on a labyrinth walk. It is different for everyone. You can sit, stand, and stay in the center as long as you want.

The fourth stage is *resolve* (Via Transformativa). It begins when you leave the center and return on the same path back out of the labyrinth. There are many aspects of this: you can resolve to take a next step in your life, or come to a resolution about something bothering you. Rejuvenation often occurs, or a feeling of rebirth begins. Or, on your way out, you reclaim those responsibilities that you set down on the way in, but you have new strength to carry them. Often a feeling of strengthening and integration occurs. Symbolically you take back out into the world what you've received. The return path is a distinctive feature of meditative walking.

I want to caution the first-time reader: the Four Rs (remembering, re-leasing, receiving, and resolving) is only a *map*; it is not the territory. You can allow blessing in anywhere on the labyrinth. You can release anywhere on the labyrinth, you can receive anywhere; you can come to resolution anywhere on the labyrinth. The Four Rs is one way of understanding what can happen on the labyrinth while you are walking. Do not hold these too tightly; during your walk you will understand the flow.

# The Basics

## No Right Way or Wrong Way to Walk a Labyrinth

The core of my teaching is that there is no right way to walk a labyrinth. I often hear of untrained leaders teaching specific things to be done in the labyrinth during meditative walking. For instance: walk slowly, don't touch others, don't stop or look down while walking in, and look up when walking out. In this way, the labyrinth becomes the project of this leader's ego. No behavior should be prescribed in the labyrinth for adults in med-itative walking. During facilitator trainings, with people who are experi-enced with the labyrinth, I invite everyone to choose a place on the path to begin their walk. Usually, a ripple of surprise moves through the group at that point. You do not even have to follow the path if you consciously choose not to!

This is important. Your spiritual life is not your own unless you create practices that nourish you. The practice of labyrinth walking is not your own if you yield to another who dictates specific behavior—you would still be following someone else's rules. The labyrinth is a sacred place set aside for you to reflect, look within, pray, negotiate new behavior, and explore your relationship with the Divine as you walk this complicated, demanding path called life. Keep it free of "shoulds" and "oughts."

## PREPARING FOR A WALK

Preparation is helpful because it begins to quiet the mind and focus your thoughts before you enter the labyrinth. However, if and how you prepare for the labyrinth walk is entirely up to you.

Preparation can be done individually or in a group. If the labyrinth you plan to walk is outdoors and requires a walk through a grove of trees, you may agree with your friends to walk there in silence. You may choose to sit quietly before entering. You may set an intention for your walk. Perhaps it is on the anniversary of a friend's death, or to celebrate a birthday. Journaling can be a significant part of your preparation if it is a helpful medium to you. You may want to refresh your memory about a specific dream by rereading your journal entry before you begin the walk.

## OFFERING SACRED ACKNOWLEDGMENT

When preparing to walk the labyrinth, or when completing it, it may feel right to acknowledge your actions in some reverential way. What you hold close to the heart is, in essence, sacred. You may make the sign of the cross, hold your hands in prayer position, or develop other gestures that express your humility, gratitude, or openness. Some actions may be meaningful habits you learned years ago; others may spring from that specific moment in time. Both are important because they connect your mind to your body to the Spirit.

## STARTING OFF AT INTERVALS

Facilitators are trained to provide a specific spacing pattern between walkers as they enter the labyrinth. If a trained facilitator is not present, allow at least one minute to lapse between you and the person in front of you.

## REMOVING YOUR SHOES

Because we began our work with a canvas labyrinth in Grace Cathedral, it seemed right to remove our shoes when we entered it. Originally the idea was to spare the canvas from dirt, but soon the act of removing our shoes became part of the activity of labyrinth walking. It felt more sacred, more reverential, to walk without shoes.

Labyrinth projects around the world usually ask you to remove your shoes to enter a canvas labyrinth. However, you do not need to remove your shoes if you need them for medical reasons. Leave them on and alert the facilitator at the entrance that you need them. Some labyrinth groups offer surgical booties to put over your shoes.

A few sponsors ask that you remove your shoes, but not to walk in your bare feet. Usually, if groups have this rule, they also offer clean socks that you return after the walk.

Removing shoes can also stir cultural differences. In France, if you are walking a labyrinth in public, do not remove your shoes. Removing them implies that you are part of a cult and you will not be received warmly.

## USING MUSIC

Many labyrinth walks can be enhanced with music. Facilitators are trained to guide the process with music as well as silence. Usually instrumental music—with a medium to slow pace—is best. If you wish, you may bring an iPod with your own music. This works well for many people.

## RECOGNIZING THE ROUTE

Occasionally a person will find herself at the entrance of a labyrinth unable to distinguish the path. I've come to call moments like these "geometrically challenged." Some people find it difficult to grasp the pattern easily. If this is your experience, ask the facilitator for help, or use a finger meditation tool, or lap labyrinth, to introduce yourself to the circuitous path before you begin to walk a large labyrinth. Most sites have them available.[2]

## FINDING YOUR OWN NATURAL PACE

Move with the rhythm that your body wants to go. This will change as you move throughout the stages of the walk. If you are going slowly because you think that is the way you are "supposed" to walk a labyrinth, you will lose your balance. When you follow your own natural pace, feel free to move around others or let them move around you. The labyrinth is designed to minimize out-in-the-world choices, but moving around others is a decision in the outer world that we sometimes need to make. Feel free to do so.

## The Path Is a Two-Way Street

You might enter the labyrinth when someone is on his or her return journey. If so, you will meet that person on the path. Do whatever feels natural. To stay with your own meditation, keep your eyes focused on the path. If you feel you want to greet that person in whatever spontaneous way—and it feels right between the two of you—do so. Doing whatever feels natural is an important guideline for labyrinth walking. It connects us to our natural flow.

## Recognizing the Metaphors

Aristotle once said that the highest form of brain function is metaphoric thinking. When we are thinking metaphorically the microcosm reflects the macrocosm. Our experience becomes a way of teaching us about the bigger picture. Let me share some examples.

People often grasp the use of metaphor when they get lost on the labyrinth. Remember, the labyrinth is not a maze. It is not designed for you to get lost in, but since you may be moving around people and meeting others on the narrow path, you can lose your concentration and step off the path. If you lose your way on the way in, you wind up back at the entrance. If you lose your way on the way out of the center, you wind up back in the center. Often people will reflect on this experience and learn something from it—"I feel lost in my life right now" or, "I needed more time at the center, so my body just took me where I needed to be." These kinds of comments are frequent after experiencing a surprise in the labyrinth.

Another example: A woman once came to Grace Cathedral's outdoor Interfaith Labyrinth after a workshop on codependency. During the workshop she decided she needed to free her inner child. This younger part wanted to have more fun and be more playful in her life. During the walk, three children came to the labyrinth as well. They were laughing as they played tag on the path. The woman grew angrier and angrier. Then suddenly she grasped the point of what was being so artfully presented to her. She was judging the children for the behavior for which her inner child longed. After her realization and a brief chuckle, she joined them in their playfulness. This is metaphoric thinking. Use everything that happens to you on the labyrinth as a metaphor.

*Disillusionment arises due to a discrepancy between the way a situation appears to be and the way it actually is.* —The Dalai Lama

## HANDLING EXPECTATIONS

You can never step into the same river twice—so the saying goes. This is true of labyrinth walking. Even though you are walking the same pattern; even though your second walk may be minutes after you completed the first—each journey into the labyrinth is different. However, if you have gained insight into your life, or glimpsed the Divine, you will want it to happen every time. An expectation may creep in. You do not realize it, but an expectation that lives beyond your awareness often determines the quality—or lack thereof—of your labyrinth experience.

When an expectation is functioning, you can easily discount your experience. For instance, you may come to the labyrinth to gain insights into an addictive pattern, yet you discount the memory that emerges during the walk. You do not realize it is a significant clue, so you leave disappointed. Discounting your experience is a common habit encouraged by our culture. It also shows a lack of mindfulness. You are not present to what is happening, nor with what Spirit is presenting to you. Labyrinth experiences are subtle and can be invisible. If you focus on what you think should be happening, rather than on what is actually unfolding, you will miss the experience.

"Experience your experience" is the guideline to handle expectations. Occasionally a workshop participant will say to me, "Nothing happened!" When I ask them to reflect on what did happen, they begin to see that they pushed away a lot of feelings (frequently irritation), thoughts, images, and interactions with others in an effort to find what they were looking for. Expectations are lenses that we put over our eyes (and sometimes our heart) so we are unable to appreciate what is occurring in the moment.

A wise person once described expectations as premeditated resentments. Frankly, the process of expectation that I am referring to is largely unconscious, so I question the word "premeditated," but it certainly can cause resentment and disappointment. This is one of the powerful lessons the labyrinth can teach. It is a practice of mindfulness. You live life to the fullest when you are present in the moment. "Experience your experience" is the teaching.

## REFLECTING ON THE WALK

Some walks can be significant and offer valuable insights. Others can be like dreaming: hazy and unfocused. Some method of nonverbal reflection can deepen the meaning of a labyrinth walk. Journaling is the most accessible way. You can bring your journal with you and take it into the labyrinth if you wish. (Remember, there's no right way to walk a labyrinth.) Drawing or sketching can be helpful. In a freehand way—don't worry if you're not a talented artist—capture any images that come to you. These methods are not meant to interpret what happened. Interpretation can extinguish the energy of the images. Instead, draw them or journal about your experience. Only later will you know intuitively what each image means. If you don't have your journal with you and there is no overt way to process the walk, keep the images in your mind's eye until you can capture them in a concrete form.

## WALKING THE LUNATIONS

The lunations are the cusps and foils that circle the outer perimeter of the Chartres-style labyrinth. You might walk the lunations if you do not feel ready to go in. They are outside the path, so you will not interfere with another's walk. Walking the lunations can provide a "warm-up" to the actual walk. Walk in the direction your body wants to go. For several months I could walk them only clockwise. When I tried the reverse, I felt uncomfortable and out of sorts. Listen to your body and let it guide you.

Walk the lunations at the end of the walk if you do not feel complete in your experience. This is a good way to complete your meditation without walking the entire labyrinth again. Walking the lunations could be understood as a method all in its own, but is most often either a prelude or a conclusion to meditative walking.

## DEALING WITH DISTRACTIONS

People comment that walking with others distracts them from their focus. If walkers are spaced well when entering the labyrinth, the distraction can be reduced. It is true, however, that a walk with just one or two people is quite different from one with ten or twenty people.

When you are distracted from your intuitive flow, you have two choices: increase your effort—not by force, however—to focus on what you are working with, or follow the distraction. (As François Legaux says, "Pray the distraction.") The distraction is taking up your

 *Pray the distraction.* —François Legaux

energy anyway, so follow it to see where it leads. Someone walking the labyrinth may have purple hair and this irritates you. Follow that irritation. What is your irritation about? Judgment? Fear? There is a lesson here that you did not expect, but if you reflect on it, it may enlighten you.

If you are pulled out of your intuitive flow, it may mean you have made a shift from a soft-eyed, receptive state into your thinking mind. If the labyrinth is crowded, or you simply can't maintain an inward focus, allow the people you are walking the labyrinth with to become the focus of your meditation. Look gently at them. Who do you imagine them to be? Who do you identify with? Is there someone in particular who draws your attention? Through this avenue, many insightful reflections about your life can be revealed.

## NOT IMPOSING AN AGENDA

There is no guarantee that what you come to the labyrinth to focus on is what is going to unfold. You may hope to work on a significant dream, for example, but it may not happen. Timing and readiness are important factors. Often your ego will attempt to dictate the outcome. You cannot impose an agenda on yourself in the labyrinth. The labyrinth supports your intuitive nature, which is often snuffed out by the task-oriented ego. The psyche has to be willing to release this intuitive information and you have to be ready to receive it.

## ACCEPTING UNEXPECTED FEELINGS

Walking the labyrinth can raise feelings that you didn't know you had. Tears may flow spontaneously. They may be tears of joy at the sheer beauty of people walking the path together. Or they may be from pain held within for a long time. You may not know why you are moved to tears. Unexpected feelings frequently happen within and around the labyrinth. Whatever the feelings are, gently stay with the experience and feel the feelings that come to the surface. Let them be present without attempting to figure out what is emerging. Experience your experience.

Experiencing your feelings can be the beginning of a healing process. You may be frozen in your life: frozen in relationships, frozen in work, and, most painful of all, frozen in your spiritual life. Feelings are the first signs that you are beginning to thaw. Once you begin to let your feelings flow, you are able to reflect upon your pain, confusion, and wounds from others. Once you begin to thaw, there is hope for healing.

Stay with the feelings until they run their course. If you were walking the labyrinth and the walk ended, you may want to walk it again, or walk the lunations. Then, in a journal, jot down the thoughts or images that occurred to you during your walk.

## ENCOUNTERING EXHAUSTION

I have seen people enter the labyrinth feeling energized and then experience a profound sense of exhaustion during the walk. This does not happen often, but it happens frequently enough that I want to draw your attention to it. If this happens to you, I suggest staying with the walk, difficult though that may be. If this profound sense of exhaustion lasts after the walk, go directly into the labyrinth again. Going back into the labyrinth does not sound very appealing to someone in this state. But my sense is that the psyche is working through something very important even though you may not know what it is at the time. If you are in a retreat center where it is convenient to go to sleep, you may choose to take a nap. Pay attention to your dreams because they may give you a glimpse of what you are moving through.

## BEING COMFORTABLE WITH THE WALK

Once you are comfortable with the simple act of walking a labyrinth, you can choose the way you want to use it. "Comfortable" means that you have walked it enough to make the experience your own. You do not fear losing your way and can smile at yourself if you do. You are comfortable moving around others either by walking faster on the longer sections of the path or turning on the turns at the same time the person in front of you does. You know the basics about shoes, music, etc. You are tuned in and curious about your unfolding experience. All this can happen within one walk. One gift the labyrinth offers is that it is easy to do. When you are comfortable, you are ready to consider specific applications.

*Four*

# Applications

*There is no right way or wrong way to walk the labyrinth.*

The labyrinth invites you to tailor your walks depending upon what you need at a particular time. This chapter offers suggestions for accessing the intuitive, in-between world that can open to you in the labyrinth. Feel free to modify them in any way while you are in the labyrinth.

## Be Open

Go into the labyrinth with an open heart and an open mind. This is always effective. It allows concerns and issues you were not aware of to emerge into your consciousness. Less experienced walkers may want to go in open to learn the overall pattern and to surrender to the rhythm of the repetitive turns. It is also good to shift into the state of being open if something unexpected happens during your walk. For instance, you want to be alone on the labyrinth but a group of people is there before you. If you had a focused intention, other people would seem disruptive. If you are open to a broad focus, the others can be incorporated into an unexpected, but meaningful experience.

## RELEASE WHATEVER IS IN YOUR WAY

Releasing is not easy. The psyche and the body have to be ready to do so. To release feelings, accumulated muscle tension, old resentments, or a bad attitude takes focus and a willingness to do so. Many practices encourage release (including several of the exercises in part 2). Breathing is perhaps the most important one. For example, locate the area in your body that holds your life force in a frozen position and breathe into it as much as possible. Breath is an underrated healing force.

Another way is to work directly with muscle tension. If you experience muscle tension, intentionally squeeze those muscles tighter and then release them. With each release, they will relax a bit more. Be patient with yourself. Stay conscious of the sensations. Letting go can take time, so it is good to frequently revisit areas that hold chronic tension.

## A PATH OF PRAYER, A WALKING MEDITATION

Meditation and prayer are often polarized in our contentious and split culture. These two words used in the same sentence may always be a problem whenever the inner world is feared and undervalued for its ability to transform. To some people meditation is a positive action, while prayer is an embarrassment and a sign of weakness. For others, prayer is positive while meditation is frowned upon—if not

**Prayer is talking to the Divine; meditation is listening. A good conversation takes both.**

banned—because it opens the door to the interior world, which is akin to opening Pandora's box.

In actuality, meditation and prayer are different sides of the same coin. Prayer is talking to the Divine; meditation is listening. A good conversation takes both. Speaking through the voice of the being is active; you take the initiative. Listening is receptive and sometimes requires waiting and keeping quiet to receive. The practice of labyrinth walking encourages both as it invites you to step into a relationship with the Divine.

Once you enter the labyrinth and quiet your mind by finding your natural pace, prayerful thoughts may simply flow out of you. People have reported that faces appear before their eyes and they intuitively know that they are to pray for these people. One teacher saw her whole classroom appear before her, student by student, and that spurred a prayerful response for each one.

If you feel awkward and do not know how to pray but want to, there is a quick way to learn: simply "write" a verbal letter to the Divine through the voice within you as you walk the labyrinth. Address it to whatever term you are comfortable with: Dear Higher Power, Dear Father, Dear Divine Mother, or Dear Holy One. And then begin: "It's been a long time since we talked . . ." or "I've never talked to you before, but . . ."

Know to whom you pray. Divine Wisdom? Divine Mother? Mother/Father God? God? Holy One? Jesus Christ? Allah? Gracious One? If you don't know to whom you are talking, address your letter to Dear Mystery, or Unknown One—"I write even though I don't know who you are . . ." No matter how complicated or maddening this

*If we really want to pray, we must first learn to listen; for in the silence of the heart God speaks.*

—Mother Teresa

relationship to the Divine may be, the avenue of access is present in the labyrinth.

## ASK A QUESTION

I have already mentioned the importance of using a question to bring unconscious dynamics into the light of day. The labyrinth is an excellent place to ask for the meaning of a specific dream symbol. You may ask any question that you carry in your heart. You may be attempting to decide how to handle a hyperactive grandchild who gets on your nerves. Or you may be facing a choice of colleges or deciding upon a new career. Yes/no questions are the least helpful, though if you stay away from a cut-and-dried answer, an intuitive answer can emerge.

In response, you may receive in your mind's eye an image to reflect upon. Sometimes seekers hear a voice that offers clear and gentle guidance. Insights seem to arrive in two forms. One is so strong and clear that your body takes it in as well as your mind. Usually this insight is yours instantly, for the rest of your life. Other insights may gently float into your conscious mind. These feel like remembering a dream upon waking. This level of insight needs to be reflected upon and deepened through the methods (such as spiritual counseling, journaling, body work movement, artwork) you have available to you. However strong or weak it is, I encourage you to write your experience down soon after your labyrinth walk.

Some of you may tend to be overly analytical and ask questions that lead to dead ends. This is not an effective use of questions. I remember one woman went into the center of the labyrinth at Chartres and asked the question, "How long should I stay at the center?" If the answer to any question is "So what?" or "Who cares?" forget the question. It is not a significant question and will not help you along your way.

*Whether you turn to the right or to the left, your ears will hear a voice behind you saying: "This is the way, walk in it."* —Isaiah 30:21

Reflect on the question in your journal and then as you approach the labyrinth, remind yourself of the question. Then simply let it go. Find your quiet mind and find the portal to the in-between world. You may feel the impulse to walk the labyrinth very, very slowly, dance, glide like a bird, or crawl through it like a penitent. Follow the wisdom of your body, and your mind will be open to a new world. Remember, the answer you seek will rarely appear as you expect it to.

## LISTEN FOR GUIDANCE

If you ask a question in the labyrinth, listen for an answer. It may evolve out of a deep spiritual restlessness. Guidance may also occur at unexpected times to address a question you did not know you were carrying in your heart.

Listening requires a deep attentiveness to your body, your imagination, and your senses. Your body may speak to you through pain and discomfort. Your imagination may birth an image. You may hear that "still, small voice," as it is referred to in Christian scriptures, that gives you direct guidance. Receive whatever channel "speaks" up. Do not push the experience away or think you are crazy. Do not force anything to take shape prematurely. Do not interpret from your analytical mind.

The still, small voice is heard quite frequently in the labyrinth. This experience is called "audition" in the Christian tradition, though it is not talked about much. How the labyrinth encourages this kind of experience is part of the knowledge we have lost. The mystery is woven into the pattern itself.

Allow the message to sink into your awareness both during and after the walk. If you do not understand what you received, make sure to jot it down after the walk. Expand and deepen the images through symbolic work such as mandala drawing, journaling, or finger painting. (See "Follow the Clues" in "Soul Assignment.")

## WALK A DREAM

Significant dream work can be done in the labyrinth. The trick is to let the dream unfold through the intuitive mind, rather than wresting an insight from it with a controlling ego.

First, find your natural pace in the labyrinth. Take your time to see if anything else is emerging. If not, and when you are ready, gently bring the dream that you want to work with to your awareness. Review the whole dream in your mind's eye as best you can. Then, go back to the place in the dream that intrigues you the most: perhaps a moment of tension or maybe a decision that you made in the dream that seems mysterious in your waking life. Explore this juncture. Let your intuitive, imaginative mind pick you up and take you on a journey. Reflect on the people your dream mind chose to use. How old are you in the dream? What stage of your life is represented by this? Do you become older in the dream? What structures appear—your home, a school, a church? What vehicles? Savor these images, but do not interpret. Allow the dream to speak for itself.

Psychologist and author Stanley Krippner offers another method: he instructs the dreamer to review the dream as if it is a fairy tale. You can do this easily during a labyrinth walk. Just start with "Once upon a time . . ." and tell the dream from that perspective. Allow other information to emerge as you do this.

During your walk, you can also redream the dream. Use your imagination! Give the dream a different, more satisfying ending. If you parted from a dear friend in anger, imagine reconciling with that person. If you woke up shaking with fear because you met a frightening figure in a dark alley, go back to that alley and confront that figure. Talk to it. Ask it who it is. Basic active imagination methods work well in the labyrinth.

## Explore Images That Emerge

An image or memory may float up to the surface of your mind. You have a choice to pay attention to it or not. You can simply let it go, but if you dismiss it without understanding or being fully aware, you might discount your experience. (See "Handling Expectations" in "The Art of Labyrinth Walking.") If you choose to explore it, it is like catching a butterfly. Hold it gently and explore it with "soft eyes." Is it a memory? If so, go deeper and bring as much of it to consciousness as possible. To gain deeper insight, gently crack the image open by focusing fully on it. Speak to it. See if it lives in a specific part of your body and then speak with that part of your body.

I teach yearly at the Golden Door, a luxury spa in Escondido, California, which was the first to put in a labyrinth for mind-body-spirit integration. I once met a woman there who was very worried about her sixteen-year-old daughter, who was to travel to China with a group from her school. Although there would be good supervision, the mother was leaning toward keeping her daughter at home. She took her struggle concerning this to the labyrinth. During her walk, a red dragonfly landed on her. She stood quietly, observing and then reflecting upon this primordial creature. Suddenly she remembered a movie she saw as a child back in her homeland of Poland. The movie was about three young girls who found a dragonfly. They were fascinated with it and wanted to keep it for themselves. Since it was attempting to get away, the girls pulled the wings off it and it died soon after that. The mother standing on the labyrinth savored this memory and gracefully received the message: she must let her daughter go to China. She cannot pull her wings off to keep her for herself. When she returned to her room, she consulted a book on symbols. The dragonfly sometimes signifies adolescent freedom.

A fantasy is handled differently. Fantasies have an ulterior motive behind them. They are repetitive and are a sign of a stuck place—they often "squelch" rather than "release" wisdom. If you explore a fantasy you can make the fantasy stronger or wind up in a dead end. Accept the fantasy—whatever it is—and then decide the general theme of it. Ask yourself what purpose it serves. Does it make you feel safer in the face of an anxiety-producing situation? Does it give you solace or a sense of control? Does it help you look magnanimous in your own eyes? If you can find the trigger that sets off the fantasy it can become a barometer signaling distress in the interior world. The fantasy can be a key to knowing yourself more deeply.

## Use a Mantra

Mantras are simply repeated words or phrases that are often neutral in meaning. An esteemed teacher may impart one or the seeker herself may select one for its vibration and sound. Repeating a mantra again and again keeps the mind focused and attentive. You can select a new mantra each time you enter the labyrinth or use the same one each time.

It is possible to be seized by a mantra in the labyrinth. A concise, positive phrase may come to you out of nowhere as you walk. It is always a helpful, repetitive phrase that offers affirmation. If this happens, I suggest that you join it by repeating it consciously. It will disappear as quickly as it came, but it is always calming and comforting. If you can, write this phrase down. These phrases are always unique to the person. Frequently they are just what we need to hear.

## SET AN INTENTION

A labyrinth walk can be designated to a special purpose. You may prepare for an important meeting by creating a peaceful space inside yourself and imagining a positive outcome. If a friend is going into surgery you may focus on giving the person strength and comfort. You can walk the labyrinth with an intention to reduce your anger about a difficult and challenging situation. If you fear that you will handle a situation poorly, you can name what you do not want to happen. This takes the energetic charge out of it. Then you can design a way to move this concern into positive behavior. The practice of walking the labyrinth invites you to be conscious and awake enough to know what you need in order to live an effective, gracious life.

## PUSH THE ENVELOPE—TRY AMPLIFICATION

The labyrinth can help you address such nebulous concerns as the pace of your life, feeling out of balance, or unwanted patterns (for example, intentionally developing discipline in something, but periodically rebelling). For working with dreams, Carl Jung developed a method called amplification that I have adapted to use in the labyrinth. To use this approach, exaggerate the dynamic you are focusing on. If you are working to find balance in your life, for example, you might choose to walk so slowly in the labyrinth that you begin to lose your balance. Lose it, and then catch yourself. Lose your balance again and catch yourself just before you fall. If you amplify it—"play" with it—the metaphor becomes literal and you can feel it in your body. In this way you may learn a great deal about the issue on an intuitive, nonverbal level. Hidden feelings that serve as the glue to hold your unhelpful patterns in place may come to consciousness.

Another example involves the struggle to allow discipline in our lives. Many of us rebel against discipline. In the labyrinth, the highly structured path can serve as both the experience and the metaphor of discipline. "Push the envelope" by moving through the labyrinth without following the path. While doing this, notice the thoughts and feelings that occur when you do not follow the structure set before you. What do you gain? Is there joy in the rebellion?

You must be conscious of the issue to amplify it. You must know what you are working on. If you choose it, you are in charge—and therefore able to explore the metaphor.

As a counterexample, a woman at a workshop took great pride in the fact that she did not follow the path. She did it a second time, walking all over the labyrinth. For some reason, she kept checking in with me to let me know that she did not follow the path. During the remaining minutes left to walk the labyrinth she alerted me that she was going to walk it again. I suggested that, for the final walk, she follow the path. She did not, and then it dawned on me—but not on her—that she probably was in some way *unable* to follow the highly structured path. This was confirmed when her friend told me that this woman was simply repeating what she does in her highly undisciplined life. Such common behavior: When we don't see the issue, we cover it up with pride or some other feeling that keeps us oblivious of the true work we need to do.

## Do a History

When you want to understand a person or an event from the intuitive, reflective levels of your psyche, do a history. This is a specific way to explore the dynamics of a relationship, be it with a person, place, or thing.

Let's say you feel hurt and betrayed by a dear friend. First, it is important to ready yourself—perhaps by walking the lunations, journaling and collecting your thoughts before you enter the labyrinth, or quieting your mind during the walk.

When you feel ready, go back to the very beginning of your relationship. "Doing a history" means gathering in your mind's eye the experiences you shared with this person. What was your initial attraction? What did you enjoy together? What was your friendship based on? These experiences can be helpful to getting to the root of the hurt you feel. Journal these thoughts or talk with a friend after the walk. What was your role in the betrayal? Were you naïve? Too trusting without enough information? The more we learn, the more we value even the most difficult experiences.

Remember you can never impose an agenda on yourself in the labyrinth. Do not force yourself through an exploration without being ready and receptive. If is does not feel right to explore what you had hoped to, then simply let it go and try it again at another time. Be receptive to whatever occurs, and later you may realize that it contains some insight you were seeking.

## CREATE A BODY PRAYER

The labyrinth invites you to let go of thoughts and enter into the world of the senses. Your body may want to be expressive in the labyrinth. You may want to dance, crawl, or skip and twirl. Allow yourself to go through a process of movement guided by your feelings and impulses. When you complete it, you may sense that you have been praying. Be thoughtful of others in the labyrinth. Refer to "Reconnecting with Your Body" in the "Healing" chapter to deepen this concept.

*We began as a mineral.*
*We emerged into plant life.*
*And into the animal state, and then into being*
*human . . .*                          —Rumi

## USE THE SIX-PETALS FOR MEDITATION

The petals are unique to the Chartres-style Eleven-Circuit Labyrinth and they have many meanings embedded within them. Besides being symbolic of the six days of Creation, each petal has a different vibrational quality to it. As you stand at the entrance of the center, going around the petals clockwise from left to right, the first on the left is symbolic of the mineral kingdom. The second is the plant kingdom. The third is the animal kingdom. The fourth is the human kingdom. The fifth is the angelic kingdom. The last has many names: the Unknowable, the Unnameable, the Mystery, the Unmanifest, or, in esoteric terms, the kingdom of conscious beings.

You do not need to know what symbol a petal represents when you're in the labyrinth. You can look up the symbolism later. Simply follow your body. When you enter the center, allow a petal to choose you and go there to meditate if possible. If there is another person in that petal, go there in your mind's eye. See what is offered there. It is important that this not be a process of the thinking mind, but an intuitive calling forth to what may need attention in your being.

You can use the petals for a specific focus or intent. If I want to check in with my health, I go to the mineral petal. If I have a friend in the hospital, I go to pray in the human petal. If I am working to bring an idea into physical form, I go to the Unmanifest petal. Make up your own method as you gain experience with the labyrinth.

## Use the Center as a Sacred Place to Share

The labyrinth can help those who have difficult things to say to one another—people who want to speak of things so tender and so vulnerable that surrounding themselves in sacred space can be beneficial. For example, six religious sisters decided to use the center of the labyrinth for a conversation about sexuality. Ordinarily this conversation would not be encouraged or allowed in their order, but these women felt that it was an important part of building community. Before they began, they agreed on some ground rules: absolute confidentiality and the content would never again be referred to once they left the center. When they were ready, they walked to the center and each sat down in a petal. After all arrived, each took the time she needed to share her upbringing and experiences. The experiences were received in silence. When each had had her turn and all were finished sharing, responses were permitted. The conversation lasted for several hours and was drawn to a close in a prayerful way and the sisters followed the return path out of the labyrinth.

> *Experience is not what happens to you, it is what you do with what happens to you.*
>
> —Aldous Huxley

## ENCOURAGE CREATIVITY AND INNOVATION

Perhaps you are working on a creative project that demands a great deal of your mental energy. Walking the labyrinth every day can restore mental energy and renew your creative resources. It can serve as a place to ventilate your thoughts. To be receptive to this, imagine that there is a great river running through your mind and body. Allow any images that come to you to flow through your mind. This will cleanse, restore, and refresh you.

Walking the labyrinth can also ignite your creative fire and awaken your muse. It can move you deeper into your creative process. During the walk, allow any images to emerge. You may want to focus on where you feel stuck or in a quandary as to what steps to take next. When I was writing *Walking a Sacred Path*, I frequently reached an impasse on how to organize my thoughts. I would walk the labyrinth, reviewing in my mind specific points I wanted to make. Though I felt little resolve during the walk, the next writing session would offer an organizational structure that suited the material. It was a wonder-filled process!

## WALK FOR STRESS REDUCTION

Hospitals and clinics are using the labyrinth to reduce stress. The simple act of walking can renew and refresh the tired staff, the fearful patient, and the burdened family. I suggest going in open for this walk if you are new to the labyrinth. Tune in to the pace your body wants to go and follow those impulses. Do not burden yourself with other "work" during a stress-reduction walk. However, if some image or insight comes

*The goal of renewal is not "freedom from stress"; the goal of renewal is new capacity: It is freedom for stress.* —Donna Schaper

to you in the labyrinth, note it. It may be a clue to disengaging from the stress you are experiencing.

## WITNESS A WALK

Often people prefer to witness a labyrinth walk, rather than participate directly through walking. I use the word "witness" rather than "watch" because "witness" implies being soft-eyed and nonjudgmental about what is happening before you. Labyrinth walks are often beautiful to witness. Witnessing can also be a way of preparing for the walk.

· PART TWO ·

# Specific Uses for Healing and Transformation

*If there are teachings associated with this new spirituality, they will be about our own psyche—much as Buddhism is. It will be a contemporary teaching, and deal with things such as how the ego develops, how we derive our sense of identity, how we create unnecessary fear, how we interpret or misinterpret our experiences, and how we can free our minds from these various constraints. They will be psychological teachings, rather than teachings about deities and other such entities.*

—Peter Russell, *The Consciousness Revolution*

Something extraordinary is happening with the labyrinths at Grace Cathedral and the hundreds of similar sites that have been established around the Western world. People are finding peace and focus in their lives. They become grounded in their bodies. Stress melts off their shoulders. And as strangers meditate—walking together, elbow to elbow—they become connected in invisible and nonverbal ways. The labyrinth is unique in how it meets people where they are and nourishes them according to their needs. The winding path of the labyrinth offers images of healing and hope. It offers steadiness and reliability when we are filled with fear and doubt. This gracious path can challenge us when we are simply drifting through life. And it can open our hearts and our minds to the extraordinary gifts of the imagination through which we can glimpse the Holy.

Author and visionary Peter Russell makes an important observation: The new spirituality that is emerging in the West will be psychological in nature. It will teach about the depth of the psyche. This remains unfamiliar territory to most of us, and yet, the psyche determines the outcome of our lives as we live them. Russell lists several areas of learning: how the ego develops, how we derive our sense of identity, how we create unnecessary fear, how we interpret or misinterpret our experiences, and how we can free our minds from these various constraints. I want to add more to his list: how the shadow—that which remains unconscious—impedes our spiritual growth; how a healthy, well-functioning imagination can guide us; and how the unhealthy, unhealed imagination can but distort our vision. We also need to know how to enter the imaginal realms. We need to learn these skills as spiritual beings walking a human path.

Unfortunately, Western culture maintains a split between the imagination and the body, and the fragmentation does not yield wisdom. At present, the rational mind is thought to be the only way to learn and develop understanding. The imagination is denigrated ("it's only your imagination") to the point where it has no credibility. Dismissing Spirit and maintaining definitive boundaries between mind and body—a central value of rationality—doesn't serve us when it comes to healing and transformation.

The Medieval Eleven-Circuit Labyrinth predates the Cartesian thinking embraced by the Western world when it moved into the Enlightenment. The labyrinth was created from a consciousness that did not divide the mind from the body and the body from the Spirit so it is able to offer a map to spiritual wholeness. This worldview understood that psyche and soma are one. Image is embedded in sensation and the marriage of image and sensation offers its own profound wisdom. Of course, since most of us identify with our culture, the West, we can bring this same split into the labyrinth. I enjoy teaching how to reconnect the division we carry within ourselves—this process is explained in the next few chapters.

Being in the labyrinth is like aqua aerobics compared to exercising on land. Because of the buoyancy of the water, you can move more freely and stretch in ways you cannot stretch on land. The same is true in the labyrinth: it offers the world in between, the imaginal world. In this realm, you can have a flowing, embodied conversation with your body, your mind, and your Spirit. Your world becomes transparent to you and you can feel the presence of the Divine, if you invite Her to be there. This is an intuitive process most people have a feel for once they are in the labyrinth. Profound, connecting insights and "aha" experiences will resonate in the sensations of the body, the psyche, and in the spiritual realms all at once. This is what the word "psychospiritual" hopes to capture, though words are limited in this realm.

The fewer levels of the psyche and soma involved, the less impact the insight will have on you. If you have an insight on the cognitive level, it will help you understand something, but it may not change your behavior. If you have a psychological insight, it may be helpful, but if it is not connected to your feelings the change can be limited. You need to venture into the land of paradox and mystery that lies just beyond the reach of the everyday world. It is important to activate as many levels in your being as possible—your conscious awareness, your emotions, your body, your thinking as well as symbolic mind—when seeking healing and transformation.

Chapter 5, "Start Where You Are," is a self-assessment to help you grasp where you are on the path. In it, you will explore your sense of self and your relationship with your family, your friends, your community, and the Divine. You will also explore your expectation of where you feel you "should" be on the path. This chapter is intended to help you reflect upon your successes and failures as well as recognize any repeated patterns that are not working for you. It is intended not only to stir reflection, but to be informative about what is working for you and what is not. You will find there a quick questionnaire with places to jot down your thoughts as you prepare for the four chapters that follow.

Chapter 6, "Healing," contains several exercises for you to look over—find an exercise that speaks to you and then take that to the labyrinth. The next two chapters, "Shadow Work" and "Soul Assignment," are related. I use the term "shadow" to describe unclaimed qualities that we have stowed in our unconscious. Some aspects of the shadow can get us in trouble, and we deal with this in the shadow work chapter. Or the shadow may stop us from finding our soul assignment; so in chapter 8, I offer exercises to help you discover your path to be of service to the community. This section ends with chapter 9, "Initiatory Rituals," which identifies six different ways the labyrinth can be used. It also guides you on how to create a ritual with the labyrinth.

The exercises in this part of the book are not recommended if you are walking the labyrinth for the first time. Get comfortable in the labyrinth first through meditative walking and the suggestions outlined in "The Art of Labyrinth Walking."

# Five

# START WHERE YOU ARE

*You have to acknowledge it before you can change it.*
—Dr. Phil McGraw

I took a drawing course with Frederick Franck several years ago. I was a novice and drawing is not a talent of mine. Yet, when he placed a head of robust green broccoli in front of our class to draw, I took up the challenge enthusiastically. The outline was easy. But to capture the flower of this vegetable, I drew what seemed like thousands of little curlicues, then some circles, and when my hand got tired, some dots. I was enjoying myself, but when he walked by to see my work all he said was, "You are not drawing what you see, but what you think you see."

I compared my drawing to the lush broccoli sitting on the table. He was right. All my dots and curlicues were representations, but did not capture the reality of the broccoli. The same can happen with your life. You can think you are living a very successful life, but if you turn around and really look, something may be staring you in the face that you refuse to acknowledge. Perhaps your debt is growing, your spouse is having one too many drinks too often, or your youngest child is manifesting a behavior problem at school. If you are not acknowledging a problem, or if you're underestimating its consequences in your life, you will not be able to change it. Most insidious are addictions: if you are under the power of an addiction, you have to acknowledge it before you can begin to work with it. Naming it will not solve it, but it's a start.

The same applies to your feelings of failure. You may feel that overall, your life is a failure. You are not accomplishing what you set out to do. You are unable to find an avenue for your talents or you made faulty decisions and are paying the price. You can be so absorbed in negative feelings that you cannot see the love in your children's eyes or the patience in your spouse standing beside you. You cannot make changes until you acknowledge what is actually taking place. Again, not what you think is going on, but what is actually happening.

The labyrinth is a larger-than-life metaphor of the spiritual journey. It calls you to trust the path and to experience directly what is happening. The path, the turns, the center, and all that you encounter on the walk have something to teach you. It asks that you be present in the moment. Walking the labyrinth is a method of mindfulness; the activity of walking calls you into presence with yourself.

In the moment before you begin the symbolic journey, there is a pause.[1] In this moment collect yourself, breathe, and notice your feeling state. If you are in pain or conflict, scared or anxious, acknowledge it. If you are joyous and grateful, acknowledge that. In this transparent world the labyrinth offers us, you can see your struggle. You can see what calls for rejoicing. But you will not be able to understand your experience in the labyrinth if you are in a state of denial, unconscious expectation, or disconnection from your emotional or physical well-being.

Let this chapter serve as the pause before you begin. It offers simple exercises—mostly quick journaling of thoughts—to get a clearer sense of where you are in your

*It is in the recognition of the genuine conditions of our lives that we gain strength to act and our motivation for change.* —Simone de Beauvoir

life. It brings into focus your own personal history, your relationships with yourself, your body, your family, friends, and community. It offers questions to draw your attention to your potential and to your relationship with the Holy. It offers an opportunity to reflect upon your successes and failures and any unproductive repeated patterns. This chapter is meant to "stir the pot" and help you to reflect on your life. The exercises are in a progression, so you may want to complete them in order. If you do not gravitate toward exercises, do only the ones that interest you.

## Exercise: Time Line

**Step 1:** Create a time line of your life. Get a large newsprint pad, or take several sheets of paper and place them end to end and tape them together. Draw a solid line across the paper. Start with zero on the left and at the other end, extend the line at least a decade beyond your present age. Start by marking decades, leaving space between so you can write in significant life experiences. Place significant turning points on the time line. Note the significant people you met. Place on the time line when you met your spouse or partner, a significant mentor, when your children were born, and any other significant happenings in your life.

**Step 2:** After you capture this on paper, look broader than the decades and name the periods of your life both physically (college, for instance) and spiritually (lost and searching).

**Step 3:** Focus on one or two of the most challenging eras. What made it tough? In retrospect, what supportive elements were missing?

_____

_____

_____

**Step 4:** What is the name of the period you are in now? What do you need now to move through this time gracefully?

_____

_____

_____

## Exercise: Checklist to Gauge Where You Are

Answer the following questions by jotting down the first answer that comes to mind. You have three choices: yes, somewhat, and no. If you get stumped on a given statement, put an asterisk by it and jot your thoughts on it in the place provided. This exercise is for your eyes only. You do not need to share it with others.

*I've been trying for some time to develop a lifestyle that doesn't require my presence.*

—Garry Trudeau

**1. Relationship with Yourself**

|  | YES | SOMEWHAT | NO |
|---|---|---|---|
| I enjoy time alone with myself. | ○ | ○ | ○ |
| I can focus my mind when I need to. | ○ | ○ | ○ |
| I watch television frequently. | ○ | ○ | ○ |
| I get away with things. | ○ | ○ | ○ |
| I love animals. | ○ | ○ | ○ |

Jot down any reactions or thoughts about the above statements:

_____

_____

_____

Write down what you have going for you, and what you feel you lack:

_____

_____

_____

> *Mr. Duffy lived some distance from his body.*
> —James Joyce

_____

**2. Relationship with Your Body**

|  | YES | SOMEWHAT | NO |
|---|---|---|---|
| I am aware of sensations in my body. | ○ | ○ | ○ |
| I overeat to comfort myself. | ○ | ○ | ○ |

| | YES | SOMEWHAT | NO |
|---|---|---|---|
| I enjoy my body. | O | O | O |
| I worry about my health. | O | O | O |
| I am an active person. | O | O | O |
| I am a sedentary person. | O | O | O |
| I drink too much alcohol. | O | O | O |
| I exercise regularly. | O | O | O |

Write down your reactions to the above statements:

_____

_____

_____

Finish the following statement: *My relationship to my body is . . .*

_____

_____

_____

### 3. Relationships with Others

#### A. Family

| | YES | SOMEWHAT | NO |
|---|---|---|---|
| I fight with my family. | O | O | O |
| I get along with my family. | O | O | O |
| We all know what the others are doing. | O | O | O |

|  | YES | SOMEWHAT | NO |
|---|---|---|---|
| I am (was) closer to my mother. | O | O | O |
| I am (was) closer to my father. | O | O | O |
| We talk a few times a year. | O | O | O |
| We talk often. | O | O | O |
| I blame my parents for problems I have. | O | O | O |
| I ignore personal information they give me. | O | O | O |
| I am a good listener. | O | O | O |

Write down the names of every family member who is significant to you, then quickly add three adjectives about each and put a plus sign if you feel they add positively to your life, or a minus sign if they are a burden in your life.

_____

_____

_____

_____

Write down any reactions or thoughts about the above questions:

_____

_____

_____

> *A friend is someone who knows the song in your heart and sings it back to you when you forget how it goes*
> —The AIDS Project Quilt

| B. Friends | YES | SOMEWHAT | NO |
|---|---|---|---|
| I have many friends. | O | O | O |
| I have a few good friends. | O | O | O |
| My friends don't truly know me. | O | O | O |
| I feel isolated from others. | O | O | O |
| My friends get me in trouble. | O | O | O |
| My friends nourish me. | O | O | O |
| I feel lonely a lot of the time. | O | O | O |
| I am competitive with my friends. | O | O | O |
| I ignore personal feedback they give me. | O | O | O |
| I get defensive easily. | O | O | O |

Write down the names of the friends who are significant to you, then quickly add three adjectives about each and put a plus sign if you feel they add positively to your life, or a minus sign if they are a burden in your life.

_____

_____

_____

_____

_____

Write down any reactions or thoughts about the above questions:

_____

_____

_____

| C. People You Don't Know | YES | SOMEWHAT | NO |
|---|---|---|---|
| I am hard to get to know. | ○ | ○ | ○ |
| Every stranger is potentially a new friend. | ○ | ○ | ○ |
| Generally, people irritate me. | ○ | ○ | ○ |
| I like to stay by myself. | ○ | ○ | ○ |
| I don't like parties. | ○ | ○ | ○ |
| I love parties. | ○ | ○ | ○ |
| I don't trust strangers. | ○ | ○ | ○ |

Write down any reactions or thoughts about the above questions:

_____

_____

_____

### D. Community

| | YES | SOMEWHAT | NO |
|---|:---:|:---:|:---:|
| Community is a great joy. | ○ | ○ | ○ |
| I feel I belong to a group. | ○ | ○ | ○ |
| I know whom I can rely on in case of an emergency. | ○ | ○ | ○ |
| I am alone and feel disconnected from others. | ○ | ○ | ○ |
| I have been disappointed, so I keep my distance. | ○ | ○ | ○ |
| I am afraid of those who live around me. | ○ | ○ | ○ |

Write down any reactions or thoughts about the above questions:

*When you come to the edge of all that you know, you must believe one of two things: there will be earth to stand on, or you will be given the wings to fly.*
—Author unknown

_____

_____

_____

_____

_____

_____

### 4. Developing Your Full Potential

*A. Expectations and Hopes*

| | YES | SOMEWHAT | NO |
|---|---|---|---|
| I am more successful than I imagined. | O | O | O |
| I have not met my goals yet. | O | O | O |
| I have no goals for my future. | O | O | O |
| I am disappointed in myself. | O | O | O |
| I have had a lot of curveballs in life. | O | O | O |
| I am angry at life. | O | O | O |
| I feel like I'm making it. | O | O | O |
| I do not expect a lot of myself. | O | O | O |
| There is no purpose to life. | O | O | O |
| My situation is someone else's fault. | O | O | O |
| I am repeatedly disappointed in myself. | O | O | O |
| I am repeatedly disappointed in others. | O | O | O |
| I am right where I expected to be. | O | O | O |

What are your greatest successes?

_____

_____

_____

What have your successes taught you?

_____

_____

_____

What are your greatest failures?

_____

_____

_____

What have your failures taught you?

_____

_____

_____

| *B. Gifts* | YES | SOMEWHAT | NO |
|---|---|---|---|
| I am aware of my gifts. | O | O | O |
| I am using my gifts. | O | O | O |
| I have not been able to use my gifts. | O | O | O |
| I am blocked at every turn. | O | O | O |
| My gifts are rare in the world. | O | O | O |
| The world doesn't want my gifts. | O | O | O |
| I am a dreamer, not a doer. | O | O | O |

Write down any other thoughts you have:

_____

_____

_____

| C. Challenges | YES | SOMEWHAT | NO |
|---|---|---|---|
| I like challenges in my life. | O | O | O |
| I have had too many challenges. | O | O | O |
| I do not feel challenged in my life. | O | O | O |
| I am afraid I will not measure up to a challenge. | O | O | O |

Jot down any thoughts that you had during this section:

_____

_____

_____

_____

*If God brings you to it,*
*She will bring you through it.*
—Twelve-Step saying

### 5. Relationship with the Holy

| | YES | SOMEWHAT | NO |
|---|---|---|---|
| I am on a spiritual path. | O | O | O |
| My path is not yet defined. | O | O | O |
| I shy away from anything religious. | O | O | O |

|                                              | YES | SOMEWHAT | NO |
|----------------------------------------------|-----|----------|-----|
| I have been hurt by organized religion.      | ○   | ○        | ○   |
| I have been hurt by New Age spirituality.    | ○   | ○        | ○   |
| I have never addressed that hurt.            | ○   | ○        | ○   |
| I believe in a divine force.                 | ○   | ○        | ○   |
| My religion does not work for me.            | ○   | ○        | ○   |
| My spirituality is vague and unstructured.   | ○   | ○        | ○   |
| I want to believe, but can't.                | ○   | ○        | ○   |
| Religion is a crutch.                        | ○   | ○        | ○   |
| I want to know the Divine, not just believe. | ○   | ○        | ○   |
| My religion is incompatible with social action. | ○ | ○      | ○   |
| If God is like a parent, I'm in trouble.     | ○   | ○        | ○   |

Write down any thoughts you have:

_There is no human act that cannot be hallowed into a path to God._ —Martin Buber

_____

_____

_____

_____

## 6. Identifying Repeated Patterns

| | YES | SOMEWHAT | NO |
|---|---|---|---|
| I bounce checks frequently. | O | O | O |
| I go up and down in my weight. | O | O | O |
| I have been fired more than once. | O | O | O |
| I have bad luck with _____. | O | O | O |
| I get drunk every so often. | O | O | O |
| I fight with people frequently. | O | O | O |

Write down any reactions or thoughts about the above questions:

_____

_____

_____

Repeated patterns are important to become aware of and understand. See the section on repeated patterns in "Shadow Work" to further this work.

Take what is useful to you from these exercises to the labyrinth. You may want to walk in gratitude for what you have in your life. Or perhaps this section has stimulated a question for you to take into the labyrinth. What is important is that you start where you are in your life—not where you think you should be, or where you want to be, but where you are.

# Six

# HEALING

*Healing may not be so much about getting better, as about letting go of every-thing that isn't you—all of the expectations, all of the beliefs—and becoming who you are.*

—Rachel Naomi Remen

Hospitals and wellness and retreat centers are constructing their own labyrinths at a rapid rate. They help reduce stress and serve as a place where one can muster new strength. They offer a blue-print for connecting the mind, body, and Spirit to support the forces of healing.

The healing that most frequently happens in the labyrinth is psycho-spiritual. Although there have been some reports of physical ailments improving in the labyrinth—especially with eye problems and joint pain—research needs to be done to document this. Psychospiritual healing fo-cuses on the interplay between the psychological and the spiritual. For example, if you have been deeply hurt by another and are carrying that unresolved hurt and anger within you, it will inevitably take its toll. It may affect your physical well-being, as well as damage your relationships. You

*"I believe I experienced healing in Grace Cathedral. After almost ten years of not speaking to my family because of childhood wounds (they had no idea where I was living), I was able to re-establish contact with my mother this spring. The voice came from my heart that I should do this. How could I not obey?"* —Aletheia Morden, Venice, CA

may repeat a litany to yourself in the silence of your thoughts, "How can I trust anyone?" The psychospiritual healing process releases anger and hurt. It then addresses the act of forgiveness.

Whatever drains our life force or revisits us in the wee hours of the morning needs healing. Whatever is not working for us in our lives needs attention. Answer the following question:

What needs healing at this point in your life? Or, what is not working for you emotionally? physically? spiritually?

_____

_____

_____

The following section offers exercises that can be done in the labyrinth to address specific areas of healing. Choose the exercises that most relate to you.

## Perfectionism

*Aim for success, not perfection. Never give up your right to be wrong, because then you will lose the ability to learn new things and move forward with your life. Remember that fear always lurks behind perfectionism. Confronting your fears and allowing yourself the right to be human can, paradoxically, make you a happier and more productive person.*

—Dr. David M. Burns

Perfectionism is a crippling problem for untold numbers of people, robbing them of what David Burns calls the "right to be wrong." Perfectionists live their lives hoping for approval. They fear they cannot measure up to the standard in their minds necessary to receive this approval, so they stop taking risks and curtail their spontaneity. As a result the perfectionist has notebooks full of unshared poems and closets full of unfinished paintings. Since the perfectionist is afraid to take risks, life is lived in the safe boundaries of appropriateness.

One woman came to walk the Grace Cathedral labyrinth struggling with the realization that her upbringing had taught her to be a perfectionist. The labyrinth reflected back to her another way of being. She wrote: "My reflections reminded me that I'd never perceived my life as being on a path. Instead, it was like I had been held against a measuring stick. And certainly it would never have been a path to center. Center would have seemed 'bad/evil' and would have needed to be avoided so I could follow the 'external measurement' of how I was doing. Those measurements would determine my worth; how I measured up. As you can see the insights from my walk are gifts to carry with me as I continue my journey."

Perfectionism differs from excellence. Excellence is when you set high standards for yourself and then do your personal best to meet them. You want to play the best tennis game you have ever played. You want to formulate your ideas so others can understand them. Of course you want your home to be beautiful and efficiently run so it can be a welcoming respite for your family. You want your children to do well in school and in life. But perfectionism becomes a tyrant when you sacrifice what is actually happening in the world to how you think it should be. You become enraged with yourself for playing tennis poorly on one occasion. If a

*Screwing things up is a virtue. Being correct is never the point. . . . Being right can stop all the momentum of a very interesting idea.*

—Robert Rauschenberg

child's play time—in the space designated to it—is curtailed because it is messy and chaotic, then your standards limit you and don't serve your children. "If it is worth doing, it's worth doing poorly" is an important guideline for a perfectionist. Remember, very few things in this world are perfect, least of all human beings.

## Exercise for Perfectionism: Amplification

Walk the lunations until you feel ready to enter the labyrinth. Once you enter, find your natural pace. Give your mind ample time to quiet. When you are ready (and that may take an entire labyrinth walk), imagine that the structure of the path is the very structure in your mind that limits you. You must stay within the path no matter what! Walk the path slowly and meticulously. Tempt yourself with the thought of stepping out of the boundary of the path. Play with losing your balance, but regain it just before you stumble across the boundary of the path. Imagine breaking the rules of this exercise. Let this be delicious to you. Be tempted to break the rules. Note any feelings, thoughts, memories or images that come up for you during this experience. What rules do you follow internally? You may want to stop at this point to write your insights before doing the final part of the exercise.

Last, begin to walk all over the labyrinth, not following any path. Break through the strictures in your mind as you step over the lines that divide the labyrinth's path. How does it feel? Play with this experience. Have fun!

Dance! Afterwards capture your thoughts and feelings in your journal. This experience may put you in touch with critical voices. If so, the next exercise may also be helpful to you.

## Critical Voices

Critical voices live in all of us, even though we may not be consciously aware of them. As you grow, the architecture of your psyche is formed by your experiences, and you internalize both the loving people as well as the critics in your life. The part of you that collects memories of critical voices may remember your parents and other significant people in their worst, scolding moments. Or, if you lack such memories, you may only hear your own critical voice installed into the software of your mind.

Your inner critics will remain silent as long as you do what they want you to. However, the less you challenge the critical voices, the more control they have over you. Once you begin to initiate new behavior (such as in the exercise on perfectionism) they can be awakened instantaneously. Once you challenge them with change, their cackle will grow louder and perhaps crueler. You have a choice here: you can give up and stop the new way of being in the world or engage them with firm, clear statements of what you need to move forward.

To befriend these critical voices seems more of a woman's challenge than a man's. Perhaps because men are encouraged to challenge the culture and stand a bit outside it, women are taught to fit into the social mores: be a good girl; a helpful, thoughtful wife. The critic inside your head can seem so much a part of you that you do not realize it is a destructive force. Even

*We so often see ourselves as failing, but God sees us as only rising, and me thinks God has the greater insight.*
                              —Julian of Norwich

after you outgrow the situation in which the voice was formed it will remain with you unless you bring it to consciousness and challenge its grip on you. Perseverance is an important quality to cultivate when working with your inner critics. Think of it this way: if your critical voices are awakened and cackling, you must be doing something right!

Often the critic is confused with the wise guidance from the "still, small voice" within that is frequently heard in the labyrinth. The "still, small voice" is soft, gentle, and encouraging. It whispers to you. It fills you with hope and invites you deeper into the mystery of life.

Critical voices are not soft; in fact they are loud and repetitious. They nag. Critical voices discourage us.[1] They take away hope and imprison us through threats and painful attacks. Here are some of the messages workshop participants have reported hearing from their critical voices:

- What will people think?
- You're too big for your britches!
- Stupid!
- You're not smart enough to accomplish that!
- Don't draw attention to yourself!
- Let the man (or woman) win!
- You are taking up too much space (or time, attention, etc.).

List the messages from your critical voices:

_____

_____

_____

Working with your critical voices is a challenge. Even though you may dislike them intensely, the psyche created them to protect you and to keep you functioning even under the most difficult circumstances. They are survival tools. The good news is that you probably no longer need them. The bad news is that they still reside in you and are often in charge of your behavior. One important law of the psyche is that you cannot change a part of yourself by attempting to snuff it out or kill it off. To transform it, this part must be befriended and understood.

## Exercise: Working with Critical Voices

Enter the labyrinth when you are ready. Find your natural pace. When and if it feels right, bring to mind a message from one of your critical voices.

Listen to the message as an observer. Whose voice is it? A parent's? A humiliating grade-school teacher's? Locate the source if you can. If the critical voice has a direct source you are conscious of, you may choose to do a history (see "Do a History" in "Applications") and move into a direct dialogue.

Another approach is to counter it from your own interior voice of strength. Accept this legitimate voice and firmly yet gently confront the critical voice. Talk to it. Thank it for guiding you in the past and wish it well. Let the critic know gently that things are going to change. Tell it you plan to allow more leeway for yourself and that you need its tenacity and perseverance to work with you to develop more flexibility within.

This exercise will help you become better attuned to your own inner voice. Your thoughts are just part of who you are and they flow through you rapidly every minute of every day. You want to switch the point of identification, to allow yourself to tune in to your thoughts from another perspective. Become sensitized to the messages you give yourself.

## Grief

The labyrinth is one of the best experiential tools available to process grief. The act of walking can be very soothing and can encourage the release of feelings that need to be experienced. In the broadest terms, grief may be said to have two forms: simple and complex. Simple grief is straightforward: you have lost someone you love, or who had tremendous impact on your life. You need to bid that person farewell whether it is because of death, a geographic move, or a severing of the relationship.

In complex grief, conflicting feelings block expression of your feelings. Perhaps you both loved and hated the person who died. Or perhaps you were unable to be present for them when they were ill and guilt has frozen your feelings. In complex grief the process can be delayed for a year or two—or even longer—so the feelings are much harder to identify and release.

Both forms of grief can be addressed in the labyrinth. The circuitous path, which turns left and right, can feel like a rocking cradle and give comfort. Remember that you are in charge of the experience. It if becomes too intense, you can walk out at any time.

Usually the emotions evoked in the labyrinth walk will not carry over to the next walk. We may feel joy or gratitude, but if we enter it again right away, our experience will most likely be quite different. The one exception to this is when grieving. If your grief is "fresh" and you are ready to grieve, tears can flow throughout several walks. The important thing is to never force these feelings, neither in life nor in the labyrinth. Be present with what comes naturally.

## GRIEVING YOUR OWN DEATH

One of the most frightening realities is the prospect of facing your own death. All of us know intellectually that we will die. We will leave the physical body and our lives will end. All of us have an expiration date, and most of us do not know when that will be. Some of us may be living with a life-threatening illness, which takes more of our time and energy to cope with as it gains and finally encroaches on our life force, our Spirit.

A woman who had a friend near death was walking the labyrinth. She heard the "still, small voice" guiding her to bring her friend from the hospice to the labyrinth. Since he was in a wheelchair and his energy was waning, she enlisted a friend's help and brought him to the terrazzo labyrinth in the meditation garden at Grace Cathedral. As she silently wheeled him along the circuitous path, he said good-bye to and thanked his body. It was a painful, tearful experience for the three of them. His death ended his suffering earlier than expected. They thought he had about three to six weeks left to live, but he died peacefully about three days later.

Dying a good death is a mystical teaching in Christianity. To die a good death means that you come to terms with your ending. You wrap up your unfinished business and live your days in the present as much as possible. You thank those you love; you reconcile your disappointments; you thank the Spark of life that has sustained you. You find a place of peace within, knowing that you will die, that everything ends, and that your happiness and strength come in not denying this fact, but in gentle acceptance of this sad reality. You can grieve about having to let go of your life and your loved ones. You can find this acceptance walking the gracious path of the labyrinth.

## OTHER FORMS OF GRIEF

Grief is not always associated with the loss of a loved one. Perhaps you lost a job you loved and you will never see your colleagues again. Or a friend has exiled you from his or her life. Perhaps you lost your home due to misfortune and the move has demanded major life changes that involve other losses as well. Or you are experiencing the effects of an aging parent's confusion, or you yourself are losing some capacities due to aging. The labyrinth is a place where these feelings can come out. New resolve can arise by surrendering to the feelings; if you allow yourself this release, you can gain new energy and new momentum.

## Exercise: Grieving the Death of a Loved One

In the labyrinth the veil between the worlds is thin. As odd as it may sound, you can carry on a conversation with a loved one in the labyrinth. You may even feel their presence with you there. You may express your love, your relief that their suffering is over, and bid this person good-bye.

If you walk the labyrinth with the specific purpose of grieving, walk in, find your pace, and then begin to reflect upon that person. Grief is layered. It comes in waves. In simple grief, allow the feelings to come. Or if the feelings happen unexpectedly, accept those feelings and allow them to flow.

In complex grief, you will need to focus your intent on grieving. Bring the deceased person to mind as well as the circumstances around your relationship. Invite that person to walk with you in your mind's eye. Say what you need to say. Never force your feelings, but allow them a safe environment to begin to flow forth. It may take several labyrinth walks over a period of time to connect with your feelings. Record the process by journaling thoughts about the deceased, including the complexities of the situation, to encourage more feelings.

Remember that the grief process is very deep and personal. Everyone has to find his or her own way. You are not crazy if you connect directly with the deceased person, or feel their presence in the labyrinth. It happens, and deep healing can occur. Do not share this with anyone who will not understand that this experience is possible.

## Forgiveness

Forgiveness is a quality we need to cultivate in ourselves if we are to live more fully. Forgiveness is misunderstood in Western culture because we place far too much faith in the mind's abilities. We think that just because we should—or want to—forgive someone, we can. If only it were that easy. Forgiveness is not dismissing memories to forget an incident. We can kid ourselves that we are done with an experience, and yet find ourselves wishing that person ill and carrying resentment and hurt. Forgiveness is a process that takes place over time. The labyrinth is an excellent place to release anger and soften hard hearts.

Forgiveness has many faces. This section is organized to address the different situations that arise. The first part is an exercise in forgiving another person who has hurt you in some way. If you are holding something against someone, it grates on your soul and drains your life force. You must tend to the roots of your hurt. Reconciliation is the obvious next step, so the exercise on forgiving another person is followed by an exercise in reconciliation.

## Exercise: Forgiving Another

Enter the labyrinth. Find your rhythm so your mind begins to quiet. Then, gently, bring the person who hurt you into your mind. This cannot be an agenda of the ego, and it may not be possible to do on your first walk of the day.

Move through your history with that person in your mind's eye. (See "Do a History" in "Applications.") How did you meet him or her? What brought you together? What did you like about this person? Bring forth the significant memories you have. This may take some time. You may want to journal about this before, during, and after your labyrinth walk.

Review the incident or circumstances that brought tension or betrayal into your relationship. Review what happened step by step. Call to mind the things that were said. Recall any "odd" statements you did not understand at the time. Imagine the other person's point of view. Imagine how he or she understands what happened. Let yourself have your feelings: hurt, anger, fear, compassion, softness—all may surface.

Feel these emotions to their fullest. Don't run from them. When we exhaust these feelings, they transform. Walk with them. Anger can soften into regret; fear can shrink and courage fill its place. Disappointment can finally coalesce into renewed commitment to live life fully. We can find the strength to take our next step.

## Exercise: Reconciling with Another

Our human instinct is usually to repair our relationships and restore connections with family and friends to a comfortable level. We want to "bury the hatchet" and live together with respect. Discernment is important here not only about how to do this, but whether it is even wise to attempt to do so. Certain life circumstances are best left alone. If you want to initiate a process of reconciliation, you must be clear on your part in causing the hurt. You cannot approach another person who holds on to the victim role. Nor can you hold a self-righteous attitude when you approach another.

Unfolding from the exercise above, ask yourself these questions:

- Was the hurt intentional, or simply part of two human beings living life?
- What was my part in it?
- Is this relationship redeemable?

- Can I involve this person in the healing process?
- Would that be wise? (There is no "should" here. Be realistic as to the situation.)
- Am I holding on to this because my pride is hurt?
- Am I still harboring anger?
- What steps do I need to take to resolve this issue for myself?

  —Letting go?

  —Writing a letter to this person that I will never send?

  —Writing a letter to be reviewed by another and then sent?

  —Calling that person?

When you have decided how to handle the situation, complete this sentence: *I resolve to . . .*

_____

_____

_____

## SELF-FORGIVENESS

One of the heaviest spiritual burdens we can carry is the inability to forgive ourselves. If some incident or circumstance is left unresolved, it can leave us vulnerable to our inner critics' tenacious hold in the form of self-attacks. There are three degrees of severity:

The first is a lack of self-acceptance. You can be too hard on yourself, peppering your internal comments with "should": You *should* be more of an expert in your field. You *should* be a more effective mother (but you don't seem to notice that you are fully committed and amazingly present to your children). Your guilt is tied in with your feelings of inadequacy, so you may always feel behind and inferior and never as if you're up to par with your peers. In the therapeutic world, this is called neurotic guilt. There is no basis for it, but you feel it nevertheless. If you have low self-esteem because you never had the traits that were accepted in the magic circle of parental love, then you may need to work hard at self-acceptance.

The second degree is when you are truly guilty of some action that needs forgiveness. This is called authentic guilt.

The third level—"being hollowed out"—addresses irreversible situations you may have caused that resulted in loss, injury, or damage.

The following exercises are focused on self-forgiveness in these three areas. Choose the level that fits your situation, though it may be helpful to read through the other exercises to gain perspective.

## Exercise in Self-Forgiveness: Level One— Neurotic Guilt

After you enter the labyrinth, when your mind is quiet and you have stepped out of your ego into the in-between realm, gently ask:

What am I holding against myself?

As suggested in Applications, do a history on it. When did it begin? Is it the voice of a parent saying you "should"? See it from many angles. Review in your mind what your supportive friends/spouse/significant

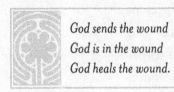

*God sends the wound*
*God is in the wound*
*God heals the wound.* —Twelve-Step saying

other have said or would say about the situation. Another person's perspective can be very helpful when we lack self-acceptance.

What do you need to do to come to terms with your lack of self-acceptance? Listen deeply while in the labyrinth. What do you hear?

Do you need to make a decision to get professional help? (If you find yourself back at "square one" yet again, then consider reaching out for help.)

Capture your experience in your journal.

## Exercise in Self–Forgiveness: Level Two— Authentic Guilt

The second level of self-forgiveness is more straightforward. It stems from your truly having done something wrong. You need to recognize it and make amends. This parallels the fourth step in Alcoholics Anonymous. The task needs to be done for your own peace of mind. When you need to repair a relationship, it takes courage and humility. In the labyrinth:

• Do a history. Review the situation in your mind.

• Name the people involved and exactly what you did wrong.

If admitting this is shocking, breathe into it. Accept it as best you can. Let the pain come into consciousness. Do not push it away.

What have you done to help heal the situation? (Apology, acknowledgment, etc.)

Is this concern only your opinion? Have you checked out your perception of your behavior with an understanding friend or therapist?

What, if any, actions need to be taken to absolve the situation?

Is it realistic to think that the people involved can be contacted?

Complete this sentence: *My plan is . . .*

_____

_____

_____

## Exercise in Self–Forgiveness Level Three— Irreversible Situations

The third level is when something in life has happened that is irreversible. You may have been the driver in a car accident in which someone was maimed or killed. You carry a heavy burden. The only recourse is to accept this painful burden as part of your life path. Nothing can take away the pain of regret and remorse you feel, so you must surrender to it. This is what I call "being hollowed out." There is nothing to do with the pain but carry it, and in doing so, you are humbled. You are emptied, brought to your knees and forced to surrender to an intolerable situation that you must find some way to live with. You may have to let go of some of life's offerings because the burden is so heavy and the energy it takes so demanding. Through this path of burden, you can become wiser, more compassionate to others' suffering, and learn never to judge another human being.

In this situation, walking the labyrinth can provide the spaciousness inside to sustain the sorrow. It can strengthen you. It can offer comfort in the midst of regret and sorrow. If you feel that living your life is a form of punishment, the practice of labyrinth walking can help you hollow a place within your soul so you can find compassion for yourself. Perhaps the best resolve is to make a life commitment to a cause or dedicate time and money to a service institution. You may create a scholarship or memorial fund in the name of the person injured or lost.

*Healing is a creative act, calling for all the hard work and dedication needed for other forms of creativity.* —Bernie Siegel

Being hollowed out can happen in more transitory ways. For instance, perhaps your spouse is dying a painful death or your father is institutionalized with Alzheimer's disease and is on the verge of not recognizing you ever again. Walking the labyrinth can be a comfort in these sorrowful times that demand a sustaining strength.

## Reconnecting with Your Body

One cornerstone of integrating mind, body, and Spirit is based on the relationship you have with your body. A conscious and obvious trauma like a car accident is an identifiable reason for healing work to occur. However, if you have been on the receiving end of physical or ritual abuse or if you were raised with a significant lack of physical touching and comfort, you may not have a solid "home base" in the world. Your relationship to the world can be tenuous and unsteady. And yet, you do not have obvious ways of understanding the injury you carry. This is a difficult awareness to allow in. But if you lack the ability to accept bodily pleasure, experience significant gaps in your ability to feel, remain sealed off in your mind and live only from the neck up, then you need to look into this with a professional companion.

The fact that there is no outside reference makes it difficult. It parallels what it feels like to be a first grader who cannot see the blackboard. There is no way to step behind someone else's eyes to see what he sees. There is no way to step into someone else's body to experience sensation. You are on your own when it comes to your relationship with your body.

The body does one of three things: it stores energy, dissipates energy, or transforms energy. We all store energy. We hold our painful experiences in our cells and some of this is held in the form of habitual tightness that may produce chronic muscle pain. We want to begin to dissipate this stored energy.

I had this principle demonstrated to me a few years ago. Every time I would step into a labyrinth, I would get a sharp pain in the first joint of my left big toe. I did not experience this outside the labyrinth, but it was very painful during my labyrinth walks. This made me very curious. I went to the center of the labyrinth to explore it further. I put my fingers on both sides of the joint. Not a split second later, a memory blossomed in my mind! I was amazed at the immediacy of it.

When I was about six, my family was involved in the yearly harvest of apples to make cider. We were working outside with the cider press on the picnic table. I was sitting near the press and was so young my feet didn't touch the ground. I lost my balance and fell, hitting my head on the corner of the slate slab that stabilized the table. I had quite a gash on my head, and my parents stepped in and took care of me. What I remember most was a neighborhood kid telling me that I was going to have a scab on my head that was going to grow over my eyes and blind me. I panicked and cried even more. I had not thought of that experience for years. This memory had been stored in my big toe. Since it was released, I have not had any pain in my toe.

As adults, we can choose how to work with our energy. When your body "speaks" to you in the labyrinth, listen. Focus on the sensation whether it is an aching shoulder muscle or the grumbling of your intestines. Ask, "What is your message?" And pay attention! See what images or memories come to mind. This will help dissipate the energy stored in your tissue. Freeing this energy will allow more flow. This energy is available for other things that will unfold in surprising and unexpected ways.

## Exercises to Reconnect with Your Body

### 1. Authentic Movement

When the body expresses itself, it becomes revitalized. Authentic Movement, a method developed by Mary Starks Whitehouse, is a very effective way to reconnect with the body both inside and outside a labyrinth. Authentic Movement is a process of listening to how your body wants to move and acknowledging those impulses through spontaneous action. Reaching high and stretching, or bending low and crawling—any movement spurred through awareness—releases the body in important ways. By exploring these impulses, you open up new life on the cellular level, in your muscles and other tissue. It is enlivening work. The freed energy gathers momentum and serves as the basis for a breakthrough that can transform your life.

Be thoughtful of others if the labyrinth is crowded. If you want to dance, crawl, or skip through a labyrinth, wait until there are only a few people walking with you.

## 2. Focus on Sensations

A second way to reconnect with your body is to direct your attention on the sensations in your body. Feel your feet on the path. (Usually this is easier in your stocking feet.) Hone your attention like a laser beam throughout your body and *experience* the sensations you feel. Do not discount anything you experience. Sensations can be very subtle; your awareness of them can be hazy. Whatever happens, experience it.

## 3. Explore Pain

A third way to use the labyrinth walk to reconnect with your body is to explore the messages you receive through sensation. This is the method I used with the pain in my toe. People sometimes report an unusual pain or ache when walking the labyrinth. Some of these experiences are simply the act of consciously recognizing a sensation that you have been ignoring. Other times, it is your body "speaking" to you in a unique way. If you experience a pain or ache, focus your awareness on it. Remember to ask, "What is your message?" The cells that store energy may release an image or a memory so that new life force can flow in. Many people feel refreshed, relaxed, and peaceful after a labyrinth walk. It is a powerful vortex that can help us release stored energy. This is subtle work and some people feel relief from the pain they experience in the labyrinth. Others do not, but they have more conscious information available to them to explore.

Labyrinth experiences build upon each other. After a healing experience, notice if any new and life-giving behavior crops up. Perhaps you speak your mind more freely, or you feel less self-conscious when speaking to a group. Or maybe you don't get irritated as quickly and find a well of patience you didn't know you had. Your connection to the Divine may also feel stronger or more stable. Accept these changes as gifts. Healing in the labyrinth is not always a conscious process.

Please remember, walking the labyrinth is *your* practice. Tailor its use to your needs. If there is anything in you that needs further healing, you will eventually come to it if you are truly on the Path. The body longs to reconnect with the Spirit and the psyche longs to heal. Many forces are inviting us to wholeness, and the labyrinth is a place where we can focus these forces of Light and consciousness to further our healing.

# *Seven*

# SHADOW WORK

*Until you learn to name your ghosts and to baptize your hopes, you have not yet been born; you are still someone else's creation.*
—Maria Cardinal, *The Words to Say It*

The biggest challenge in spiritual work is working with the shadow. Even though some people may bristle at the word, everyone has a shadow. Carl Jung defined the shadow as the unclaimed parts of ourselves that we cannot allow into conscious awareness. This information contradicts who we understand ourselves to be, so we automatically push it into the unconscious. It is important to note that the shadow contains our gifts and talents that we are afraid to use as well as the unattended business—the underbelly—that accumulates as we struggle toward maturity.

Your shadow can be active in any part of your life. For example, you may have the respect of your colleagues because you handle people well, but when you get home, you have outbursts of rage over insignificant things. Or you may be an excellent income earner, but you forget to pay the phone bill so many times that the phone company cuts off service frequently, creating an embarrassment for your entire family.

Since the shadow resides in the unconscious, we cannot know about how it is functioning until our life circumstances begin to reveal obstacles that make us fail. We are not able to secure what we want and need for ourselves. Usually we project onto others what we are not able to allow into consciousness—both the good qualities and the difficult ones. Our task is to engage it as soon as the shadow emerges through dreams, images, or painful life circumstances. One person who was "bit" by the labyrinth began to receive speaking invitations from a variety of groups wanting to hear about her work with dreams. She was terrified of speaking, and yet she mustered the courage to say yes to these invitations. By accepting the invitations, she was engaging the shadow and calling it forth. (The exercises in chapter 5, "Start Where You Are," are designed to help you begin this process.)

In this chapter on shadow work, you will look at what is *not* working in your life. This way you can get glimpses of your shadow, of what hinders you and sabotages your relationships with others and often with the Divine. (The next chapter, "Soul Assignment," will explore the positive yet challenging areas of the shadow that can guide you to find your passion and connect you to your life force.)

If your shadow is unattended to, it will stalk you. Eventually you will feel stuck in your life. In my spiritual direction work with others, I have noticed that there seems to be yet another rite of passage for many at the end of the second third of life. Much is made of the famous midlife crisis, but I also see a threshold many people come to— especially women in their late fifties—

*You are the veil that hides the paradise you seek.*
—St. Brendan

where they cannot move forward. They feel stalemated by life. The damage from old wounds reawaken in the icy light of shadow and hobble them.

You don't have to seek out your shadow. It lurks below the surface and will make itself known as your life unfolds. The trouble is, you may not pay attention to it in the milder stages. Finally, its force may surprise you when it is too late to repair the damage. It may be too late to save a marriage because your spouse is fed up with your infidelity. It may be too late to be hired for a creative job you wanted because of bad references that confirm, to everyone else but you, your unconscious authority issues. It may be too late to find common ground with your teenage son. The only thing you can do then is to learn from your mistakes and disappointments and keep a keen eye on what is not working. You need to listen to unbidden feedback from others, although it may be painful to receive, for it could hold a truth to consider.

Your shadow loses its power as you bring it to consciousness. Once you allow it to enter your consciousness, you gain insight from it and therefore you grow. New parts of your personality emerge and you become more honest with yourself and more authentic in your relationships. However, because you have new experiences, meet new people, and take on different challenges, the cycle will begin again. The shadow will reorganize itself in these new territories in ways you don't expect. Shadow work calls for a lifelong awareness and is the fuel for your creative evolution. It is the cornerstone of your spiritual growth.

The first step to working with the shadow is the most challenging: to accept

*One does not become enlightened by imaging figures of light, but by making the darkness conscious.*

—C. G. Jung

that you have responsibility and accountability in everything you do. This includes everything that happens to you, because you play the major character in your own drama. If you don't take responsibility, you project the problem onto other people and this places you in a victim role. Someone else is to blame. Someone else took actions that offended you. Jung said, "That which we do not bring to consciousness appears in our lives as fate." The shadow wants to come to the surface because the psyche wants to heal. Use the exercises in this section for reflection and to engage your shadow. It will help you deepen your compassion, increase your patience, decrease your judgments, and sustain you as you serve the world.

## Exercise on Engaging Your Shadow

To locate where your shadow is active, use the questions below to look at the circumstances of your life. Your answers in "Start Where You Are" may be helpful in the following exercises. Take the time you need to reflect upon the following question (for your eyes only):

What part or parts of your life are not working? (Writing this down is not a commitment to change it, only to acknowledge it.)

_____

*Wisdom is never violent . . . where wisdom reigns there is no conflict between thinking and feeling.*
—C. G. Jung

_____

_____

_____

_____

If what you wrote fits one of the categories below, then explore the exercises there. If it does not fit, tailor the exercises to meet your specific needs.

On a scale of 1 to 10, rate the satisfaction you have in your relationships (10 being the most satisfied):

**1. Spouse or Significant Other (if applicable)**                    **Rating:** _____

What concerns remain unresolved between you?

_____

_____

_____

**2. Close Friends**                    **Rating:** _____

Is there any concern that remains unresolved with one or more of your friends? Is it the same or a related issue?

_____

_____

_____

**3. Broader Friendships and Community**                    **Rating:** _____

Are you isolated from community, or are your interactions superficial when you are with others?

_____

_____

_____

Is the same concern repeated in each of the answers you have given?

_____

_____

_____

Write down any information a spouse or partner or close friend has given you about yourself that you have not listened to, deny, or don't take seriously:

_____

_____

_____

## Exploring Repeated Patterns

Repeated patterns are very important to pay attention to, especially unproductive ones. Repeated patterns of negative or destructive behavior are signs that something is not working right in your life. Binge drinking, bursts of rage, compulsive gambling—these patterns are easy to identify. Subtler ones include procrastination and passive-aggressive behavior, such as failing to tell your spouse you're going out for the evening when she went out of her way to cook a special dinner. Human behavior is very complex, and recognizing a repeated pattern is an effective way to gain insight into what arena of your life your shadow is at work in. Engage your shadow by following the clues it is giving you. Again, the shadow wants to be recognized and assimilated into a whole, well-working psychospiritual system.

## Exercise for Repeated Patterns

Dedicate a labyrinth walk to reflecting on a repeated pattern that you have identified in your life. Walk in, allow your mind to quiet, and then reflect upon the repeated incidents that have caused you trouble. Each will have different circumstances around it, but the behavior will be the same. It may be in the area of financial failure or in broken relationships. If you have lost your job three times in four years, then review each circumstance. Do a history of these situations (see Applications). This may take several walks. Write down in your journal the behavior that comes to your awareness. Further the work by sharing your experience with a trusted friend. Consider working with a psychotherapist if the behavior has been over a period of years.

## Being Stuck

Your shadow can corner you and make you feel at an impasse: Things do not pan out. Hopes for the future dim or turn into mirages. No matter what actions you attempt, you wind up at the same place again. When you feel stuck and are not moving forward with your life, most likely you need to engage your shadow. This is a good time to use the labyrinth regularly.

## Exercise for Being Stuck

Set aside a regular time to walk the labyrinth. It may be every day or once a week, but allow it to be a regular time for at least one month. This way your psyche begins to rely on that time to reveal itself. Once your mind quiets, focus on the feeling of being stuck. Where do you experience it in your body? What muscles are holding you in that pattern? Pay close attention to what emerges in your mind's eye. Remember that your psyche wants to heal itself; it wants to move forward in an organic way. So allow yourself to reap the harvest of each labyrinth walk. Pay close attention to your dreams. Walk any dream—or fragment of a dream—that you have during this time (see "Walk a Dream" in Applications). You may want to take your journal with you to record thoughts, images, and memories that emerge as you walk. You may also want to engage a therapist or spiritual friend in this process if the sense of being stuck continues beyond a month or two after initiating this work.

*We have not understood yet that the discovery of the unconscious means an enormous spiritual task, which must be accomplished if we wish to pre- serve our civilization.*     —C. G. Jung

Record your impressions here:

_____

_____

_____

# Unconscious Override

A surprising experience can happen in the labyrinth that can help you engage your shadow. Over the years of observing this I have come to call it "unconscious override." Even though the basics of labyrinth walking are easy to do, you may override them to reveal to yourself some other lesson.

In a workshop recently, a woman new to the labyrinth heard the basic information on labyrinth walking. But when she met someone coming out of the labyrinth on her way in, she thought that she was doing it "all wrong." Even though she had heard the facilitator say that the path is a two-way street—that you will meet people who are coming out as you go in—she did not absorb it. She exited the labyrinth with a sense of defeat and failure. When a friend reminded her that meeting people on the path is a part of meditative walking, she could see that this experience reflected back to her a basic fear that dominated her life: the fear of making a mistake.

Her unconscious "overrode" the guidelines so she could begin to see that she lived her life in the shadow of this unconscious fear. These important experiences, of things that seem like "mistakes," yield rich insights when we reflect upon them. This is where the guideline to "use everything as a metaphor" is very instructive.

Note here what surprises you have experienced in the labyrinth:

_____

_____

_____

# Self-Care

How you care for yourself can reveal elements of your shadow. You may think of yourself as hearty and believe you will never be sick, so you are careless with your health. You push yourself to work hard for long hours at a time. You are driven—perhaps because you hold a grudge against yourself and cannot find a gentle place inside to resolve it. This is more common than you may think. Reflect upon your motivation. There are an infinite number of ways to disregard difficult and unresolved feelings. We may have to prove ourselves by being better than everyone else. Or we may feel unworthy so we never say what we need, but become resentful that our needs are not taken into consideration. Addictions certainly offer a variety of ways to keep these feelings in the unconscious. You can overwork, overeat, or drink too much. As Emily Dickinson wrote, "Narcotics cannot soothe the tooth that nibbles at the soul."

As you age, caring for yourself becomes more important. What do you need to do to maintain or increase your self-care? Repeated patterns abound in this area, so you may want to use the exercise on repeated patterns offered above.

## Exercise for Self-Care

Enter the labyrinth and allow your mind to quiet. Then begin to explore this concern. Gently ask yourself questions such as: What area of self-care (having fun, getting enough sleep, seeing friends, eating well, minimizing addictive behavior, etc.) do I do well in? What area am I weakest in? Am I struggling with an addiction—a repeated pattern—to food, work, drugs, or sex? What do I need to do to succeed in coming to grips with it?

Record your insights into these questions. What will lead you into healthier behavior?

_____

_____

_____

## The Reflective Mirror:
## Dealing with Irritating People

Life can be full of irritations. You may hurry to the ATM and find it is out of deposit envelopes, or be stuck in rush-hour traffic on the way to an important meeting. The day may hold many irritating circumstances. But if another human being is irritating you, ask yourself why *that* person, why *that* behavior, and why now? When you are attached to your thoughts and identify with them, you may not realize that the behavior that is irritating you has something to do with you.

All spiritual disciplines teach the art of seeing through the ego. If someone is bothering you—whether it is mild irritation, annoyance, or strong feelings of disgust—the spiritual work is to reflect upon the root of your feelings. "Perception is a mirror, not a fact. And what I look on is my state of mind, reflected outward,"[1] the Course in Miracles teaches us. Life reflects what we carry inside back to us. One benchmark of psychological and spiritual maturity is the ability to see through our limited perceptions.

Once we become aware of our projections, we can receive others as they are, not as we think they should be.

One woman came to walk the labyrinth at Grace Cathedral when she was angry with her friends. She was enraged with them because she knew they didn't care for her, so she was ready to kick them out of her life. They would not agree with her about the way she saw things so after the walk she was going to call each of them and tell them they were not welcome in her life. She was walking the labyrinth with three or four other people and as she became present to herself, she began to realize how everything looked different from different parts of the labyrinth. At first she was curious about it, and then she began to engage this insight. Suddenly her anger broke into tears. She realized that she was insisting that her friends see things exactly as she did. She expected them to walk in her shoes and when they did not, she felt they didn't care.

## Exercise on the Reflective Mirror

Enter the labyrinth and when your mind quiets, bring into your awareness the person who is irritating you. Explore the irritating behavior. What is it about it that irks you? Who else in your life has (or had) a similar impact upon you? What part of you reacts negatively to this behavior and this person? Does this irritating behavior mean something to you beyond the actual behavior? (For instance, you don't feel cared for, as in the example above, or you associate it with disrespect.) When have you exhibited this same irritating behavior?

*Every blade of grass has an Angel that bends over it and whispers "grow, grow."* —The Talmud

Note these thoughts and reflections:

_____

_____

_____

# The Judging Mind

Your shadow is often revealed through your judgments. If you remain un-aware of your thoughts, you may not notice when your mind is judging either yourself or others negatively. An acting adage says if you judge the character you are attempting to portray, you will never gain knowledge of the character. The same is true on the human stage: if you judge another person, you will never get to know them. Earlier I used Archbishop Desmond Tutu as an example. His character was overlooked due to his skin color. Your judgments serve as a filter and block out positive aspects from your awareness. Over time, your judgments can limit your worldview so that they become a self-fulfilling prophecy.

## Exercise for the Judging Mind: Practicing Soft Eyes

Judging others is not something we want to perpetuate. We need to see oth-ers for who they are, not who we think they should be. This is as true of the people we meet in our daily life as it is of people from other cultures or religious traditions unfamiliar to us. The labyrinth has taught me that if we are in a soft-eyed place, the mind has a much harder time judging.

If you are not sure what soft eyes feel like, try this: Find the most distant point in the room you are in. Or if you can look out a window, find a distant point. Let your eyes focus on a far-off tree, as if you are searching for a rare bird. This is a long-distance, or hard-eyed, way of seeing. Some people call it hawkeyed.

Next, take a moment to gently close your eyes. Pat them lightly with your fingers to remove the strain of the hard-eyed position. Open them and this time focus on the lines in the palm of your hand. To see them clearly, the lenses in your eyes must adjust. This is the soft-eyed position. It is intimate; it is close-up. It beholds softly rather than focuses specifically. This is the place where the mind can let go of judgments.

Take a walk with soft eyes. It may be in nature or in a labyrinth. Either way, allow your eyes to remain in the soft-eyed place. If you see a judgment dart across your mind, move back into soft eyes.

Allow yourself to go into the labyrinth and find your soft eyes. Reflect on a person for whom you feel love and compassion. Savor these thoughts and feelings. When you are ready, focus on someone about whom you hold negative judgments. Review your relationship with that person as you walk the path. Perhaps you will find that your judgments are defensive. Behind them you feel threatened, angry, or frightened by this person's actions. Let yourself explore with soft eyes what is truly going on in your relationship.

Write down your thoughts:

_____

_____

_____

# Control Issues

One Veriditas facilitator told me about an unusual incident during a labyrinth walk: a woman arrived at the center of the labyrinth first, and when others arrived, she instructed each person, in a rather loud voice, where to stand!

We all have control issues, but this story illustrates one person caught in the extremes of needing to control. Taking control is a way of attempting to manage anxiety. If you feel uncertain about what is going to happen, and you experience that uncertainty as anxiety, you comfort yourself by attempting to control others' behavior. The trouble is, controlling behavior does not work unless the others are compliant personalities who do what they're told.

Most often, controlling people irritate others. Controlling behavior undermines the initiative and confidence of the person being controlled. So it is a positive step when the person being controlled "rebels" to protect herself from being undermined. However, this usually leads to conflict.

It does not, in the end, feel good to be in the controlling position. People react by shying away from you, getting resentful, or digging in their heels. You feel unsupported when what you ask—or demand—is not paid attention to. It's a recipe for continuing conflict.

# Exercises for Control Issues

You can work with this in two ways: by yourself or with another person (or more) who knowingly shares your concern. This person may be controlling too, or may be at the mercy of your behavior.

**On Your Own**
If you are exploring this behavior on your own, walk the labyrinth and find your own natural rhythm. When you are ready, allow yourself to reflect on a situation in which you know you were controlling. This awareness may have come through feedback from others, or from your knowledge of your shadow. You may also use this exercise for a future event that you are worried you will attempt to control. Think about what your motivation to control is about. Do your fears get ignited? Do you feel you are the only person who will get it done properly? Be honest.

Write your reflections:

_____

_____

_____

Consider your tactics to maintain control. Do you lay blame? Induce guilt? Belittle? Perhaps you give off a simmering rage or a loud silence. Locate what it feels like in your body when you use these tactics. Bring into your awareness the pattern that you get caught in. Once you identify it, ask yourself what you need. You may need to forgive yourself and you may need the support of others to help you in this area. Acknowledging this trait to your loved ones can go a long way, too. Professional help may be needed. Journal your thoughts as you move through this exercise.

Record your impressions here:

_____

_____

_____

## With Others

To look at the issue of control with friends or family, enter the labyrinth as a group, allowing a comfortable space between you. Each person can choose where he or she wants to start on the labyrinth walk. It does not have to be at the beginning. Once your friends are settled into their walk, cross over the boundaries to another person and—without words—gently guide or even push them into walking a different path or walking faster or slower. Everyone can take a turn at being the controller. Be serious at first, though, as the exercise continues, it may become humorous and playful. This is an amplification method to get in touch with what it feels like to control and/or be controlled.

Keep track of memories, feelings, and other bits of information that are prompted by this exercise. They may help you find the underlying cause of your control issues. If your tendency to control is extreme, it is wise to get professional help.

Note your thoughts:

_____

_____

_____

Working with our shadow is the core of an authentic spiritual life. If we remain unconscious—and therefore unaccountable for our actions—we walk through life hurting others and isolating ourselves. If we continue to project onto others all that we cannot tolerate in ourselves—our hate, our cruelty, our judgments, our sexual fears—then we are adding to the conflict and divisions already tearing at the fabric of our society.

# *Eight*

# SOUL ASSIGNMENT

*Whether you be sleeping or waking, by night and by day, the seed sprouts and grows, though you know not.*

—Rule of Taizé

Walking the labyrinth quickens the Spirit. There can be an amazing acceleration of the unfolding of your path. Your calling begins to find a focus. One friend jokingly put it this way: "I began walking the labyrinth and over time I said to myself: 'Nothing is changing, nothing is happening.' But then I realized that my whole life is changing, slowly, like an axis changing position!"

Each of us has a divine pattern encoded within. I mentioned earlier Divine Entelechy or the "acorn theory" in referring to how the soul unfolds in our lives. All that is folded within that seed is waiting for the right time and the right place to take root and break ground. So, too, it is with each of us.

We are all here for a purpose. That purpose, first, is to awaken. People need to awaken to the fact that we are living on a dying planet. The human species is destroying its habitat and using natural resources quicker than they can be replenished. We need to align our lives with the life-giving forces that bring Light, healing, and peace to the world. We need to become conscious beings as we walk the earth. We need to learn how to share and respect others who are different from us.

As we awaken, we feel the nudge of a call to offer ourselves in the service of others. We know that we are here to use our gifts, but we may be unsure how, so we begin to search for ways to do so. What are you to dedicate yourself to? If the call is strong and clear, you may feel summoned to do a certain task or break open a new frontier. If you turn down these nudges, they may become more persistent. If you refuse to pay attention to them, you wind up feeling that you have not lived your life as fully as possible. Such is the unfolding nature of our Soul's Code.

The labyrinth in Chartres Cathedral is created out of 272 stones inlaid in the floor of the nave. When I began to make frequent pilgrimages there, my friend François Legaux, dean emeritus of the cathedral, told our groups that each stone symbolizes one day of human gestation in the mother's womb. At first, this seemed like a bit of French Roman Catholic piety. But over the years, it has become for me a significant way to understand the labyrinth. It is a birth canal. It is the womb of the Divine Mother. It births those who come in search of manifesting their Soul's Code. It soothes our fears and allows us to be authentically who we are. It catapults us into applying our gifts in service of all sentient beings and in service of the earth.

*The secret of life is to have a task, something you devote your entire life to, something you bring everything to, every minute of the day for your whole life. And the important thing is—it must be something you cannot possibly do.*

—Henry Moore

The labyrinth initiates the soul's organic unfolding process, which expands far beyond the specific act of walking the labyrinth. Synchronicities begin to occur and new paths open up. New people and opportunities present themselves in often surprising ways.

These experiences become avenues to a new life and a new way of being in the world.

> *What in your life is calling you?*
> *When all the meetings are adjourned*
> *And the lists laid aside*
> *And the wild iris blooms by itself in the dark forest.*
> *What still pulls at your soul?*
>
> *In between your heartbeats hides a summons.*
> *Do you hear it?*
> *Name it if you must,*
> *Or leave it forever nameless*
> *But why pretend it's not there?*
>
> —The Terma Collective

## Exercise: Focus on Your Soul's Code

What pulls at your soul? In your wildest imaginings, what do you feel you are on earth to do? (Don't judge, censor, or bypass the thoughts and intuitive "hits" that come to mind.)

_____

_____

_____

Write down the things for which you have the most passion:

_____

_____

_____

Write down what stops you from going more toward your passion:

_____

_____

_____

## Follow the Clues

Did you ever play Treasure Hunt? Someone would place clues under rocks, trees, and other hiding places and my neighborhood friends and I would have to find them, one clue leading to the next. The spiritual path can be like that. One clue leads to the next and we, like amateur detectives, need to unravel the meaning of each clue so we can find a way to use our gifts in this life.

These clues are often in symbolic form. "The soul thinks in images," said Aristotle. When the soul is activated and begins to reveal itself, it is often through images. Some clues are fleeting, but lead to the next step. Other symbols last a long time and carry us through many turns on the path. One woman saw a large red beating heart in the center of the labyrinth. She was startled and had no reference in which to understand it. After researching the image, she came upon the tradition of the Sacred Heart of Jesus, an image out of the Middle Ages that became central to a well-established religious order. This became a symbol for her that she was loved and stood in the sacred heart of the Beloved.

Images that emerge in the labyrinth are important to this unfolding process. When you are walking the labyrinth, memories can float to the surface of your conscious mind. Dream fragments can come into your awareness. Paintings that you recently saw may settle in your mind.

I use the word "images" very broadly here. An image can include a "felt sense" or an auditory prompting that you hear within your heart. Images do not have to be visual, and may be sensed very subtly. What symbols, memories, images, intuitive "hits," sensations, or dreams are revealing themselves to you at this time? Note them here:

_____

_____

_____

## Exercise: Find the Clues

Walk the labyrinth, and when you're ready, allow yourself to receive what is happening in your mind. This process is a bit like watching clouds move through the sky: as images or ideas float up, be receptive to them. Let any image speak to you. Be with it and savor it. Again, do not interpret it! Interpretation is the rational mind's attempt to understand what is revealing itself. At this stage, interpretation limits your understanding; it does not expand it.

Write down what came up during your labyrinth walk (feel free to include any image that comes up in any other meditative method as well):

_____

_____

_____

# Ground Your Fear and Excitement

When you begin to discover the clues that tap into your Soul's Code, there is a mixture of excitement and fear. The excitement is exhilarating; you feel as if you're on the right path. The pieces are fitting together and Spirit is clearly guiding you.

But you may be afraid of the activation of these forces as well. They threaten to change your life as you know it. You may need to step out of the career path you planned and choose something that your friends and family will not understand. You may need to take the risk that you have been postponing for years. You may find that your life has come to a turning point and you can no longer hold off the need to make new decisions. Your restlessness dissipates as you focus on what longs to be lived out. Such is the force of your soul assignment. Having a practice to sustain you during this exciting and fearful time is important.

## Exercise: Walk through Your Fear and Excitement

Walk the labyrinth as frequently as possible during this passage. Let it focus your attention and ground you in your body. Notice your breath as you walk. Use spontaneous movement like reaching, crawling, and dancing (see "Authentic Movement" in "Healing"). The more at home you are in your body, the more focused you will be to move through the forces of chaos, fear, confusion, and distraction.

Facing specific fears is part of the process of discovering your soul assignment. List your fears below and rate them from 1 to 10 in terms of intensity (10 being the most intense):

**Rating:**

_____    _____

_____    _____

_____    _____


Focus on the easiest one first: do self-talk around the fear. If your fear is "What will people think?" let yourself consciously state what you fear people will think and say to others. Each time you revisit the fear, it will have less power over you.

*And the day came when the risk to remain tight in the bud was more painful than the risk it took to blossom.* —Anaïs Nin

Write out the details of your fears:

_____

_____

_____


One fascinating element to consider: The strength of your fear is also the strength of your power that you keep bottled up within. We women especially are afraid of our strength and power. It terrifies us to stand vulnerable and open in our creativity. We fear that we cannot stand firmly in leadership roles or speak the truth of who we are and what we value.

The practice of walking the labyrinth can ground and stabilize you as you experience the disorientation that occurs when you tap into your Soul's Code.

# Use Your Imagination

Your imagination can be either your friend or your enemy. Learning to activate your imagination in the service of your soul assignment is an important step. Otherwise, the imagination can turn against you. For instance, you may have fleeting negative images of things that may go wrong at a special occasion you are organizing. Your fears can be magnified and you begin to imagine embarrassing moments happening. These imaginings will impede you from finding and deciphering the clues that guide the discovery process.

When your Soul's Code unfolds, you do not have control over it. What is attempting to emerge is, most likely, beyond your wildest imaginings. However, you need to take the step of imagining beyond your limited script for yourself, otherwise you will not be prepared to accept what is unfolding within you. Once the process begins to unfold, you have to rely on all the practices you have put in place. Keep putting one foot in front of the other. Do what is in front of you. Keep an eye out for your shadow. Breathe.

## Exercise: Imagine What Is Unfolding

Enter the labyrinth and let your mind quiet. Imagine what you want for yourself. Picture in your mind very specific things unfolding. Where are you living? With whom are you in partnership? What is your work? For example, are you teaching in a classroom or doing underwater research in a small submarine? During the flow of the labyrinth walk, let images move through your mind. What does your new life look like?

_____

_____

_____

Remember, you cannot control what is unfolding. This is a "flexibility" exercise that can help you more easily receive the Divine Entelechy guiding you. Know, too, that what you are imagining will not be how the Soul's Code unfolds.

## Wait Well

Waiting for your soul assignment to reveal itself is part of the spiritual path. However, waiting can be very uncomfortable. An intense inner restlessness gnaws at you, and yet you don't know what step you should take next. You can feel lost, disoriented, even angry. Waiting on the spiritual path is a discipline all by itself. You must hold steady and keep putting one foot in front of the other as you navigate this passage.

At Grace Cathedral and other labyrinth events, there may be as many as forty people walking the labyrinth at the same time. If you walk the labyrinth with this many people, a line of people sometimes forms waiting to go into the center. Waiting to go into the center is part of the experience. Use this as a metaphor. Are you also waiting on your spiritual path? If so, are you helping this waiting by honoring it? Are you doing all you can to support yourself during this waiting time? On the labyrinth, that means remaining soft-eyed and breathing comfortably. In life, it may mean increasing your self-care by allowing more pleasure into your life. How are you sustaining yourself?

Anger and frustration are often part of waiting, and expressing anger can be part of the breakthrough. You may want to find a good spiritual guide, therapist, or life coach to guide you through this period of waiting. Accept the invitations that come to you during this period, even if they do not sound very appealing. Attend workshops and conferences and treat yourself to once-in-a-lifetime experiences.

## Where You Are Is Where You're Supposed to Be

Many people come out of the labyrinth with a confirmation that they are exactly where they need to be on the path. This confirmation cannot be forced. If you experience this realization, let it sink into your awareness.

Given the information that you are exactly where you need to be, you may feel a release from pressure. Write down what you are doing to support yourself during this time (e.g., continuing to be open, continuing to make new friends, etc.):

_____

_____

_____

# Transform a Life Assignment

You may search for a soul assignment, but a life assignment is also given to some of us. You may be born into an unusual situation. Your family may be rich and powerful and have international name recognition. You may be born blind or deaf or have suffered an illness when you were young that put you in a wheelchair. Or perhaps a parent is in prison during your entire youth. The hope is to turn a life assignment into a soul assignment.

For instance, if you've been diagnosed with cancer, you may learn not only how to go through the debilitating process of chemotherapy, but also how to rely on others. Just the act of receiving can be a major challenge to many of us who pride ourselves on independence. How we find strength, how we meet these difficulties, is a spiritual challenge as well as a psychological and social one.

Aging is another challenge that everyone who lives long enough will face. How we age, and how we handle our aging, says a great deal about who we are. The idea that aging does not change us, but makes us more who we are, has a ring of truth to it. If we did not accept ourselves when we were young, self-acceptance will be hard to come by when we're old. Forgetfulness, slowing down, loss of mobility and acuity—all these become opportunities to deepen ourselves spiritually. Acceptance of the life process is the spiritual task.

Life assignments are situations that you have to learn to work with and grow from. You can deny the impact of what happens to you, or you can allow it to become your teacher. Through these experiences, you deepen your compassion for yourself and those you meet on the Path. If you do not have the support you need and the burden of the life assignment is too heavy, you can become bitter and lonely. The Dalai Lama reminds us that we have two ways to respond to difficult circumstances: we can fall into self-destructive behavior, or we can use the situation to strengthen ourselves.

## Exercise: Life Assignment

List the people you know who were given a life assignment:

_____

_____

_____

What did these people teach you?

_____

_____

_____

If you have been given a life assignment, what are you to learn from it at this stage? Have you addressed your anger, blame, and/or depression?

_____

_____

_____

# Nurture Strength and Perseverance During Challenging Times

Life demands periods of time when you need strength and perseverance. Building inner strength takes not only patience, but also conscious effort. You need to align with the part that is rooting for you and nurture it. You have to become your own best friend. Methods like healthy self-talk, journaling, increasing your time with friends, having a regular massage, and perhaps using professional help are all ways to become a friend to yourself during any demanding, vulnerable time.

Perseverance is the ability to place strength upon strength so you can sustain yourself during challenging times. You come face-to-face with perseverance when you are exercising physically at your maximum or when you are sustaining a long assignment by carefully pacing yourself. All this takes you to the depths of your soul.

## Exercise: Nurture Strength and Perseverance

Enter the labyrinth, quiet your mind, and breathe deeply. When you breathe in, allow strength to flow into your body. Breathe out and release any obstacles you feel are in your way. Remind yourself that you are a child of God and that you are here for a reason even though you may not yet know what it is.

Reflect on any self-generated attacks that undermine your efforts. Are there any critical voices cackling within you? (See "Critical Voices" in

*There is nothing enlightened about shrinking so that other people won't feel insecure around you.*
—Marianne Williamson

"Healing.") If so, answer them from your strength. Remind yourself of your short-term goals.

Ask the Divine for what you need when walking the labyrinth. Write your needs down here:

_____

_____

_____

Return to the labyrinth as often as you need to during difficult times. Review what has transpired between walks either mentally or through your journal entries so you are conscious of when parts of the challenge you face are accomplished. Perhaps you have learned more about what impact a surgery will have on you physically. Or you have just finished the first draft of the essay needed for your college applications. Perhaps you have found the couples therapist that best suits you and your partner's needs. Acknowledge your progress and continue to become conscious and ask for what you need one step at a time. If you are unsure of what that may be, start with what you know is necessary for the journey. This is a time to reach for that which sustains you.

## On the Wrong Path? Design a Transition

Your strength dwindles if you are committed to goals that aren't suited to you. The direction of your life does not unfold, but clunks along in fits and starts. It takes strength to admit to yourself that you are headed in the wrong direction. Once you do that, you can devise a plan to help yourself step away from the commitments that are sapping your life force. During the walk, devise a plan to change direction that has integrity to it. Allow this change to be honorable and, though difficult, something that you can look back upon without guilt or shame. This is a hard thing to do, so you may need to enlist a life coach or therapist to help you.

*Whatever can be truly expressed in its proper meaning must emerge from inside a person and pass through an inner form. It cannot come from outside to inside of a person, but must emerge from within.*
—Meister Eckhart

## Exercise: Designing a Transition

Walk the labyrinth as often as you can as you move through this transition. Identify—even say aloud—the names of the people or organizations that will help you during this time.

List them here:

_____

_____

_____

Find your pace; quiet your mind. When you're ready, imagine in your mind's eye what you want for yourself. Refer to the "Imagine What Is Unfolding" and "Nurture Strength and Perseverance" exercises in this chapter. Design a plan that has many small steps to it; for instance, stop working late in a job you hate and begin to use your evening time to nurture yourself, preparing for the day when you can leave.

More times than not, change has a financial element to it as well. Develop a budget and plan when making a change is feasible. This way you can gain control of not only your finances, but also your fears that may stop you from moving ahead with making a life change. Start researching the idea you're contemplating, such as going back to school or moving to another part of the country. This is a step-by-step process that will take support from others, and it will be a time of hard work, focus, dedication, and persistence. Do not reject any idea because you think you will not succeed. When initiating change, you have to put yourself on the line and let others accept or reject your actions. For instance, you may take a risk and apply to a master's degree program. Most people are pleasantly surprised.

When this period is over, celebrate the process. Perhaps you have changed jobs and started training for a new career, or left a painful marriage. At the end, you may want to choose some friends to walk with you. Consider creating a ceremony to commemorate this. (See "Honoring Rites of Passage" in the next chapter.) Walk the labyrinth one more time to reach a feeling of closure, acknowledging the hard steps that you had to take to get there. Live your new life. Do not return to the labyrinth until it calls you back (but don't forget to listen for the call).

Finding our soul assignment is hard work. The process can test our perseverance and at the same time, it can teach us skills we need to continue the journey. We learn along the way what we need to integrate, in order to continue on the Path.

# Nine

# INITIATORY RITUALS

*Ritual is food to the spiritually hungry. Ritual has the potential to heal and warm; to glorify God and reify human devotion; to make objects and places sacred; to create community; to permeate the membrane between religion and peoplehood and bond one person to the whole. Ritual physicalizes the spiritual and spiritualizes the physical.*

—Letty Cottin Pogrebin, *Deborah, Golda, and Me*

Labyrinth rituals—and, more broadly, ceremonies—can be designed to meet today's spiritual hunger. Ritual draws people together. It is a way to unify people from different backgrounds, to find common resonance, and to provide connection and understanding.

Ritual is looked down upon in some parts of Western culture. It's dismissed as boring or meaningless. In fact, some dictionaries define "ritual" as a series of meaningless acts, which was the psychoanalytic worldview from the 1960s. But ritual is slowly weaving itself back into the fabric of our world. And we are richer for it. The labyrinth is playing a significant role in this revitalization of ritual and ceremonies.

# The Old Smooth Stone and the Sacred Feminine

There are two approaches to ritual: one—named by Diane Eck—is the Old Smooth Stone method; the other is the New Paradigm approach. In liturgically oriented churches—such as in the Roman Catholic, Lutheran and Episcopal traditions—the Old Smooth Stone approach holds sway. In this approach, the order of the service remains the same though the content changes. The worshippers know exactly what is going to happen next and are soothed by the steady unfolding of the service. This allows the mind to relax and be open and receptive to what is being said, read, or sung. The ritual becomes the container for the transcendent experience. In the Old Smooth Stone approach, the leader plays a central role in leading the service, preaching, and celebrating the Eucharist.

The Old Smooth Stone is very effective and the same principles are used in different religious traditions throughout the world. Its appeal may be limited to an older generation, however, as younger people find the repetition boring. Younger people's attention is being cultivated in a vastly different way: through technology, computer games, and the predominance of ten- to thirty-second sound bites on television, Western society is teaching a form of split attention. For instance, are you irritated, or do you feel more fully informed when an anchorperson is reading the news while at the same time teletype information is streaming by at the bottom of the screen? Is it disruptive or informative? The Old Smooth Stone method does not relate to these new cultural methods although people are experimenting with this in worship.

The Sacred Feminine approach is almost the exact opposite. Rather than calming our minds by a steady, trustworthy, and familiar pattern unfolding, this method calls us into the immediacy of the moment. It is often done with smaller groups. When using the labyrinth, most times people are standing in a circle on the labyrinth at the beginning of the ritual. Often the setting is outdoors. In the Smooth Stone approach, we ignore the ambulance siren that screams outside. In the Sacred Feminine method, we acknowledge the possible trauma and suffering that the siren signals as we gather into our circle. We acknowledge the baby crying in the background and the birds chirping in the distance. The Sacred Feminine method calls us into the moment to teach us presence. In this model, a leader guides the process, which includes periods of spontaneous actions on behalf of the group. The leader carries the responsibility of helping people feel included, safe to share what they want to, and recognized as having a valuable contribution.

The labyrinth is an excellent place to experience both methods. In the Old Smooth Stone method, the path of the labyrinth is a trustworthy friend. All you need to do is focus on the path. This frees the mind to reflect upon pressing concerns and—if you choose—wrap them in prayer. I will illustrate these uses more in the section "Affirming Beliefs and Making Meaning."

The Sacred Feminine methods are used most frequently on the labyrinth. When people are gathering for a full moon walk, or to celebrate someone's birthday, friends gather in a circle in the middle of the labyrinth before the walk. They may greet one another, make a statement of how they are that evening, and state an intention for their walk.

*The purpose of ritual is to wake up the old mind, to put it to work. The old ones inside us, the collective unconscious, the many lives, the different eternal parts, the senses, and the parts of the brain that have been ignored. Those parts do not speak English. They do not care about television. But they do understand candlelight and colors. They do understand nature.* —Margo Adler

# The Roles of Ritual

Ritual is "food for the spiritually hungry," writes Letty Cottin Pogrebin. Ritual serves the community in many ways. As a therapist in New York City in the 1980s, I came across a book by Evan Imber-Black and Janine Roberts, *Rituals for Our Times: Celebrating Healing and Changing Our Lives and Our Relationships*. Much has been written since then, but this was written for therapists to help weave ritual into our work with clients. It was the first glimpse I had about the power of ritual. I have adapted this work to the labyrinth over the years. The authors outline six different ways the ritual empowers: by creating community, honoring rites of passage, grounding us in the everyday, supporting healing, celebrating special occasions, and affirming beliefs and making meaning.

## CREATING COMMUNITY

We can begin community building through ceremonies that help us relate to one another. For example, when people attend a full moon labyrinth walk every month to honor the cycles of the earth, strangers and friends come together. The labyrinth offers the chance to express shared ecological concerns as well as to get to know one another. At the beginning of the walk, usually peope take a moment to express concerns and make requests of the community.

One group gathered at a labyrinth to acknowledge the summer solstice and one member of the community was missing. The participants knew that she would not be absent without a reason; this walk was too important to her. One of them went to check on her. She was at home alone, ill and in need of help. He immediately got her to a hospital. Had she not been a member of our labyrinth community, who knows what would have happened? The labyrinth knits people together.

## The Processional Method

Another way the labyrinth can create community is through the processional method of walking the labyrinth. Sister Marie, a nun in the Community of St. Paul, taught me this method at Chartres Cathedral in 1995. It is a highly structured ritual that is a challenge to North Americans, who often find it hard to accept a structure imposed upon them. I have not heard the same kind of response from the European labyrinth community.

Here's how it goes: The participants are lined up and each person extends an arm, lightly touching the shoulder of the person in front of them. The line is formed (according to height is best—the tallest at the end) before entering the labyrinth and the leader begins the walk at a slow pace. The pace must be slow or those at the end of the line will feel as if they are playing the childhood game of whip, rather than walking the labyrinth. It is best if each person starts on the right foot, though this may not be able to be maintained throughout the walk because of the turns, which can be very challenging.

The line snakes through the labyrinth until it reaches the center. The leader then steps sideways into the left petal in a half-note rhythm, in contrast to the slower whole-note rhythm used to reach the center. The leader, keeping the rhythm, steps clockwise into the second petal while the second person in line steps into the first petal. Like the gears in a clock, each petal is filled. When the leader completes the sixth petal (the one to the right of the entrance) she steps into the center of the center, keeping the rhythm, and then out the *back* of the labyrinth, stepping on the labrys as she leaves. Everyone follows, keeping the rhythm as much as possible. The curious thing is that there is no path out the back, but it is a quick way to exit. After exiting, I have the participants move silently around the outer edge of the labyrinth until everyone has completed the walk and then do a brief ritual ending.

This method is used during the summer solstice walks at Chartres Cathedral when there are huge crowds. Walking out the back is necessary when there are hundreds of people walking the labyrinth. It is too difficult to walk out on the return path due to the long line on the path waiting to go in. At times there are so many people, with no sense of spacing, that the line snakes through several circuits of the labyrinth though people do not place their hand on the shoulder of the person in front of them.

On the solstice, I have observed many variations at the center. Sometimes people fill each petal and move around as described. Other times I have seen the line stop at the entrance to the center and only one person at a time step into it. When the person is finished meditating, dancing, or whatever she or he chooses to do, that person walks out the back and the next person enters.

Some people accustomed to meditative walking are irritated with the processional approach when they first try it. Also, it is hard to walk the labyrinth meditatively when a group is doing the processional style. It is best to get out of their way. Besides creating community, the processional method is effective in building teamwork and group cohesion.

## The Harmony Walk

I created the Harmony Walk out of my experience at Boldern Academy in the foothills of the Alps during my visits to Switzerland in the early 1990s. When walking the beautiful Baltic Wheel labyrinth—created by Susanne Kramer—I heard cowbells ringing constantly in the distance. Added to this were smaller, higher-pitched bells fastened on the collars of the sheep. It was a lovely setting in which to walk the labyrinth and the sounds of the bells still resonated within me when I arrived home. So I created the Harmony Walk, using handbells in a free-form way.

We instruct participants before a walk on how to ring a handbell: not to touch it with bare hands and to press it against the body to stop the ringing when and if they want. All the handbells (we have nine of them) are tuned to the pentatonic scale, so there are no wrong notes. The group approaches the labyrinth in silence. The appointed leader walks the lunations ringing a handbell consistently until others feel free to join in. Some participants begin to ring their bell right away, others find their pace and begin to ring the bell whenever they want. There is no specific pattern and no expectation about what may unfold. Sometimes there is silence; sometimes just one bell rings; and often times, many bells ring at once. The sound builds and begins to mesh as people begin to listen to one another. Musical patterns are created and then evaporate into thin air. This is a wonderful way to create community and people always comment about the beautiful, peaceful effect it has on both participants and witnesses.

## HONORING RITES OF PASSAGE

Rituals can help mark changes in our lives and honor transitions.

After the tapestry labyrinth was placed in Grace Cathedral, a teacher from the San Francisco Waldorf School contacted me through my friend Ellen McDermott. Twelve young women were graduating from eighth grade and wanted to acknowledge this important passage in their lives. They wanted to include their mothers in this ceremony and use the labyrinth.

Ellen and I went to work designing the ritual. We designated her as the Wise Woman. She provided two readings that focused on the challenges of growing up. Ellen and I gave instructions to the participants beforehand, then we silently entered the cathedral in mother-daughter pairs. After the first reading, I lit the candle at the center and the daughters formed a circle outside of the outer edge of the labyrinth. The mothers entered first. I stood at the entrance of the labyrinth to welcome each one, provide sufficient space between each person, and hold the sacred space of the labyrinth throughout the ritual.

Once the mothers had entered the center and taken time for reflection, each lit a votive candle from the large lit candle that had been placed there. Then, when each mother left the center by the same path, she carried the candle with her. When a daughter saw her mother leave the center, she moved from the outside circle of peers to the entrance to begin her own walk. The mother gave the candle to the daughter when they met on the path. Amid hugs, tears, and squeals of delight, the mothers and daughters experienced a memorable time.

It was a lovely rite of passage ceremony. And, as often happens, a surprise came from the experience. The young women stayed in the center and serenaded their mothers with song! As they exited, the Wise Woman read a final passage and I ended the ritual by extinguishing the candle. This elegant, poignant ritual was effective in sending these young women into the next phase of their lives.

The Women's Dream Quest is a ritual overnight event that began at Grace Cathedral in 1987 and now occurs around North America. It is an opportunity for women to sleep in sacred space together and acknowledge the passage of time through honoring the Maiden, the Mother, and the Crone. Through large- and small-group ritual and sharing, singing and movement, women have a place to express their sorrows, hopes, and visions. The labyrinth serves as the ritual centerpiece and is available all night for walking. This is a very special way to honor the aging process, to heal and to build community.

## GROUNDING US IN THE EVERYDAY

In the early 1980s, I took a course from Sister Hose Hobday, a Native American and Dominican nun, on how to create rituals that help us feel centered and walk with clarity and power through each day. As an example of empowering ritual, she described getting up in the morning and making the "perfect" cup of coffee. Each action is done with consciousness. She stays in the present moment as she gathers the water, measures the coffee, and waits until it is ready to drink.

You can be worn down by the tasks that need to be done each day. Taking a shower can become drudgery; retrieving the morning paper can become a burdensome task if we lose our sense of joy in living. But these tasks can renew you as well. It all depends upon how you embrace your life. Walking the labyrinth can bring you into the present moment. It can also reveal to you the attitude you are living out as you move through your day.

It is helpful to walk the labyrinth daily as you prepare for surgery. You can build the strength you'll need and fine-tune your attitude toward the experience. You can determine your "care circle" of family and friends and invite them to join you on your walks. Use the labyrinth in whatever way empowers you in your life.

## SUPPORTING HEALING

In the chapter on healing are many ways to use the labyrinth individually in the service of healing. When you add the element of ritual, other people may join you and serve as participants as well as witnesses to your experience. Ritual has the ability to hold paradox. It can sustain and provide a container for people feeling both love and hate, humility and self-righteousness, hope and discouragement. Below are two rituals: one is for personal healing; the other is for healing the community.

### Personal Healing

Veriditas has an online newsletter called *The Labyrinth Journal* that features "Little Miracles on the Path" in each edition. Facilitators create and share rituals through this publication. An example of personal healing comes from an anonymous walker: "My husband and I are separating after forty years of marriage. Just as we had a ceremony to celebrate our marriage, I wanted to have some sort of ceremony to provide ending and closure. My husband has seen me walking (our community labyrinth) from our apartment window and asked if he could walk as well, so we decided to walk on our forty-first anniversary. We walked in together and when we reached the center, we reminisced and thanked each other for the good memories from our marriage and said some words of forgiveness and release and wished each other well. We then walked out separately to symbolize our moving forward on our separate paths. For me, it was a meaningful and memorable little ceremony to mark the ending of our marriage."

*World Healing*

Natural disasters seem to be happening worldwide. Whether we think of the hurricanes, earthquakes, or tsunamis, we are all affected in some way. The Asian tsunami tragedy in late December 2004 captured the world's attention. The enormous destruction and loss of life seemed unimaginable. We wanted to help, so sending money as well as clothes and supplies was important. But the sorrow in our souls for the suffering people remained untouched.

On January 23, 2005, the Labyrinth and Sea Project initiated a worldwide labyrinth walk, conceived by Selma Sevenhuijsen, Carol Comstock, William Frost, and Lea Goode-Harris. Thanks to the Internet, the event was announced around the world. Hundreds of labyrinths were available where people could walk, pray, and share the burden of sorrow for the hundreds of thousands of people affected by this tragedy.

Because the destruction and loss of life was due to the death-dealing force of water, the rituals asked for the "restoration of the healing power of water." The waters on the planet are all connected and serve as a source of life and blessing. Below are three examples of rituals that occurred that day. (All are from the website www.waterlabyrinths.com.)

On the shore of Lake Zurich, Switzerland, a dozen women, brought together by Susanne Kramer and Rosmarie Schmid of labyrinth-international.org, danced around a statuette of Yemaya, the female Creator from Yoruban lore who is associated with the ocean and its treasures. Ursula Schlatter, who made the statuette, led the ritual, accompanied by a Brazilian tune sung by Nurudatina Pili Abela. Then we circled a hill in the park three times in a labyrinthian way: once turning right, once turning left, and once again turning right—for the dead, for the surviving, for the water to be healed and to heal. (Submitted by Susanne Kramer.)

Twelve people and one doggy came to walk the Chartres-style labyrinth at Ghost Ranch, New Mexico. We began the ceremony by joining hands and offering prayers for the victims, the survivors, and the water affected by the tsunami. We extended these prayers to include all the water on the planet. Each person brought a small amount of water to pour into a labyrinth fountain basin in the center. We then joined hands again to offer our blessings to the water. At this point, a huge raven began cawing in a tree just a few feet from the labyrinth. Raven is the guardian of ceremonial magic and in-absentia healing. We then proceeded out of the labyrinth, in a procession-like manner. Everyone stayed for lunch and shared their feelings about the wonderful energies that were present and all felt like we had made a difference, experiencing the magic of the Land of Enchantment. (Submitted by Vicki Keiser.)

Bell ribbons knotted in prayer for tsunami victims and survivors lined the bowl of local water from Port Gardner Bay, the flooded Snohomish River, and the chalice well in Glastonbury, England. Walkers at Wiggum's Park labyrinth in Everett, Washington, honored the power of water to give and take life. Nearby, cedar branches were used to disperse the water onto the walkers and the sixty-foot brick Chartres-style labyrinth at the closing ceremony. (Submitted by Laurie Crawford.)

This is not the only example. Other Veriditas initiatives such as the Global Healing Response that connects labyrinth facilitators to emergency efforts has recently been launched. Weekly peace walks began at Grace Cathedral soon after the United States embarked upon the war with Iraq. These efforts are to build community despite the disagreements that we share. They are to provide a healing environment for individuals and communities that are united by difficult challenges and hard times.

## CELEBRATING SPECIAL OCCASIONS

Labyrinth ceremonies affirm life and the joy of living. They bring in the element of festivity. Those invited to celebrate a special occasion at a labyrinth often dress up or come in costume to honor the event.

Croning parties involving the labyrinth are quite popular. When a woman turns sixty, she enters her wisdom years, and the term "crone" has recently been revived to describe this passage in life. These ceremonies challenge our Western cultural assumptions about women of a certain age being "over the hill" and invisible and no longer of value to the culture.

One woman, Janet, invited a group of twenty women to celebrate her passage into becoming a crone. The women gathered at the appointed time and the ritual leader, on behalf of Janet, made sure everyone was introduced before the ritual began: they gathered in the center of the labyrinth before the walk and each woman described how she had become friends with Janet.

The leader explained the ritual and blessed the labyrinth and then they all returned to the outside, by the entrance of the labyrinth. They entered the labyrinth individually, about twenty feet apart, and walked reflectively to the center. When all the women had arrived, they formed a rather large circle that spilled out of the center so they could all see and hear one another. Janet stood in the center with the leader. Each woman had written or brought a prayer, poem, or memento of appreciation to be read aloud. Candles and other small gifts were given to Janet and the readings were collected to make a scrapbook. Spontaneous hugs and tears were certainly part of the ritual. When the verbal sharing was complete, the women walked the return path back out. Everyone waited at the outer edge of the labyrinth for the others to complete the walk. An inspirational reading about being a woman of wisdom ended the ceremony. The women returned to the leader's house for refreshments and to continue the celebration.

*We need to create transformative metaphors for God that give both men and women the sense of their holistic potential, and don't just duplicate gender stereotypes on the divine level.*

—Rosemary Reuther

## AFFIRMING BELIEFS AND MAKING MEANING

The labyrinth can be used as a sacred place to share consecrated bread and wine. The service can be done around the labyrinth or as people are walking in; the scriptures can be read as people are walking in silence, and the prayers can be done spontaneously once people arrive at the center.

Rituals can highlight a specific time during the church year. For instance, many facilitators offer a walk on Good Friday. On Ash Wednesday at Union Theological Seminary, we placed a prayer bench in the center of the labyrinth. Participants reflected upon their mortality and remembered those who died that year. They walked the labyrinth, and when they reached the center, they knelt down and received the ashes on their forehead. Then they walked the path back out. This solemn, effective, but simple ritual brought new depth to the liturgical phrase "Remember that you are dust, and to dust you shall return." (Holy water can also be used at the edge of the labyrinth. If you use incense, do it sparingly. Be creative; you can also use prayer stones, angel cards, and scarves.)

Rituals knit together communities and transform them. People who are called to the present moment learn to be present with one another. They create community and create bonds between people. As Letty Cottin Pogrebin writes, "Ritual physicalizes the spiritual and spiritualizes the physical."

## Examining the Rituals in Your Life

While rituals created for the labyrinth are life giving, rituals can also set up and reinforce behavior that can be destructive to us.

Let's explore the use of ritual in your life.

List the empowering rituals you have in your life (these may be daily, such as setting the breakfast table before you go to bed, or seasonal, such as preparing for Hanukkah by taking the candles and menorah out of storage):

_____

_____

_____

Name any areas in your life in which you would be more empowered if you moved through these activities using ritual:

_____

_____

_____

List the disempowering rituals, or unhelpful habits, you have in your life:

_____

_____

_____

Note when disempowering rituals begin and how they increase in their power over you. Identify any repetitive patterns you can; search for the trigger that sets it in motion. (See "Repeated Patterns" in "Shadow Work.")

_____

_____

_____

# How to Create a Ritual

All rituals and ceremonies need to be simple and straightforward. They should not be elaborate or lengthy. If they are too complicated, the group will become self-conscious as they attempt to figure out what to do.

1. First, set your intention for the ritual. In one sentence, state what you want to acknowledge and transform through this ritual. (This is for your own planning, but may be read as a formal beginning or end to the ritual.)

_____

_____

_____


2. Decide whether you want to do this alone or bring friends along. If you are ending a marriage and a few steady friends have supported you through the divorce, you may want to invite them. Acknowledge, but do not comply with, any social pressure about whom to include.

_____

_____

_____


3. Choose meaningful symbols you want to use. What items helped to

sustain you? You could consider, for example, burning an item symbolic of the past during the ceremony.

---

4. Expand your thinking beyond symbols. What activity would you like people to participate in? Earlier I used the example of a croning party, in which guests made brief statements telling how the honoree enriched their lives, and others read poems and gave small symbolic gifts. Reading and personal statements work well in a ritual as long as they do not take up too much time.

---

5. Create a simple, easily executed ceremony to meet your intention. Begin with the structure of the labyrinth: Do you want a meditative walk to be part of it? Or do you want to focus it on the center? What activity of acknowledgment do you want people to do? Who will lead it?

---

6. Finally, make two lists to summarize your planning. Use the first to outline the procedure of the ritual. How does it start? List what happens next,

and then the activity that follows that. Do this all the way to the end of the ritual. Do not leave out any detail. Write out specific instructions that you will need to give the group.

The second list is for the supplies you will need. Think through the whole ritual process as you outlined it in the first list. Then write down all the supplies you will need, such as candles, matches, and writing paper. Rituals can go sour if you do not have the supplies you need in the moment you need them.

If creating a ritual feels foreign to you, ask someone to create it for you. This person would be the designated leader of the ceremony. The skill of creating a ritual for yourself or others develops over time. Start with small occasions until your experience grows. Veriditas facilitators are trained to do ceremonial labyrinth rituals and you can find them by calling the Veriditas office (415-561-2921), or through their website, www.veriditas.org.

Rituals and ceremonies in the sacred space of the labyrinth offer infinite possibilities! Be creative and have fun. As long as the leader is not too vague in his or her guidance, or too controlling—prescribing people's behavior—the ritual will unfold naturally and the participants will find meaning.

The labyrinth lends itself naturally to ritual and ceremonial use. Enjoy the labyrinth in this way. You will be nourished by it.

# Conclusion

# A SPIRITUALITY FOR OUR TIMES

*Your path is your own, but you must walk side by side with others, with com-
passion and generosity as your beacons. If anything is required it is this: fear-
lessness in your examination of life and death; willingness to continually
grow; and openness to the possibility that the ordinary is extraordinary, and
that your joys and your sorrows have meaning and mystery.*

—Elizabeth Lesser, *A New American Spirituality*

Hunger for the Sacred has reached epic proportions and it is manifesting itself in many ways. Terrorists are consumed with a
passion for the Divine that celebrates their own and others'
sudden deaths to earn their way into heaven. Fundamentalism—often
mean-spirited—reduces the Holy down to steadfast rules and beliefs; indeed "cutting the person to fit the coat." It is a time to call like-minded
people together; people who value each other despite differences in skin
color or cultural heritage. People who are awake to the precarious state of
our environment must come together and wake up others. It is a time to
confront the fear and violence that is sweeping the planet as humankind
struggles with dwindling resources, mind-boggling technological advance-
ments, and globalization that is changing the way we understand ourselves.

How can we find a practical spirituality that sustains our strength, deepens our respect for all sentient beings, helps us work with the shadow, and gives us clarity as we walk the Path?

The spiritual search today is guided by longing. It is a longing for the Divine. A longing to have a direct experience of the Holy, rather than simply believing in the tenets of a faith handed down to us. In the words of theologian Marcus Borg, we want first-hand, not second-hand religion. We want an experience, not just beliefs. The Buddhists embrace spirituality as "tranquil abiding." Elizabeth Lesser writes, in *A New American Spirituality*, that this spiritual longing is "neither a feeling nor a thought, it is more like a gravitational pull in the direction of wholeness, enlightenment, truth—what some call God."[1] And the reward is what author Parker Palmer calls "the rapture of being alive."

At the same time that so much violence is happening in the world, many disciplines that study human nature—such as psychology, the healing arts, psychoneuro immunology, the mythopoetic movement, research in integrative medicine—are getting much clearer on what encourages healing and transformation within the human soul. The new spirituality that is emerging is utilizing these approaches to help people deepen in compassion, change unproductive habits, and change their attitudes so they can live more fulfilling lives and serve as instruments of love and peace. The labyrinth is serving as the crucible where we can ground our spiritual longing, nourish our soul-selves, and encourage these transformative moments.

*We are called to spiritual maturity that will unveil new potentialities, no more visible in the human self today than radium was in the physical world a century ago.* —Lewis Mumford

In this conclusion I want to weave together some of these concepts we've been working with. Their integration informs us as to how healing and transformation take place within us. There is much to say but that is for another context. Here I am going to limit myself to four major points.

*1. All sacred knowledge is hidden from the everyday level of ego-consciousness.*
Though the fruits of spiritual work are lived out in the ordinary world, true spiritual wisdom is hidden from everyday life. You have to dig within to find the gems of truth that produce inner transformation. Earlier in this text, I used the image that the spiritual life is like a treasure hunt and we find one clue at a time leading us on along the way. This image is effective because it is true: We cannot have direct access to sacred knowledge. We must be ready to receive it every step of the way. There is a protection built in to guard this knowledge, and yet, during these frightening and precarious times, we need this knowledge to come forth to instruct our lives. However, if we come to this knowledge in our everyday, unprepared ego-selves, we will distort it, or use it for our own self-aggrandizement. We will use it to control others and induce harmful consequences. One need only listen to the nightly news to be reminded of the religiously motivated violence that is sweeping the world.

The knowledge is guarded to protect us as well. Direct connection with the Divine can be like sticking a finger into an electric socket. The voltage can be too great for us. We must prepare ourselves by enlivening the body, finding solid community, and allowing Spirit to transform us in the subtlest way.

We can have a raw experience of the Holy when we are in the liminal or imaginal realms. When we are in this state, symbolized by the Grail Castle, we need to be fully present in the moment and attend to that which arouses our curious and compassionate hearts. The labyrinth serves as a portal to this in-between realm.

Part of the wisdom that we seek rests upon the care and well-being of our imagination. The imagination, which is viewed with great suspicion in fundamentalist settings in all traditions, is an integral ingredient in healing and transformation. In the imaginal realms, the imagination is the faculty that recognizes the sacred. "To the imagination the sacred is self-evident," declared the mystic William Blake.

The imagination is an important ingredient for connecting to the sacred. We need to nourish it—by experiencing symbols and great art and by consciously working with our dreams. At the same time, we need to protect our imaginations from exposure to violence and destruction. We should not let our children have a steady diet (even through Saturday morning cartoons) of bombs exploding and people killing one another. The imagination and our whole inner world is nurtured by beauty in all its forms—nature, music, the arts—and the loving acts of people, both strangers and loved ones alike.

*A new human is being called forth to be a creative participant in the further evolution of life here on planet Earth.* —Robert Keck

### 2. The new spirituality is redefining many elements of religion.

The new spirituality is redefining many elements of organized religious thought. Such areas as authority, faith, truth, and the meaning of the sacred are changing.

In traditional religion, God is the ultimate authority and you must be obedient to God to walk the way of faith. Now the individual is assuming more authority over his or her life. When you pursue a spiritual path, integrating a variety of wisdom teachings, you commit yourself to honing your own sense of inner authority. We trust ourselves to mature spiritually so we can discern what is best for us. We are developing a system of inner guidance by cultivating our experiences through reflection, accountability, and openness to learning. Therefore, we must stay attentive to our mistakes and analyze what assumptions we are going by when we do not have our hopes and longings come to fruition.

To cultivate our inner authority, we need to develop our intuitive skills by following our hunches. This means persistently keeping an eye out for whether we have made an accurate assessment of any given situation. Did we truly act on knowledge given to us from within? Or did it come from unexplored experience that we cast onto another through projection? The answer to these questions comes from paying close attention to what is genuinely happening in your life and enlisting friends to engage you honestly. Do not let anyone take this privilege away from you.

The new spirituality is also redefining the faith journey. It is no longer to climb Jacob's ladder higher and higher to perfection. It is walking the path like Parzival, learning from mistakes and from the people you meet on the path as you search to find the portal that opens the imaginal realms. This acknowledges that the journey to God is unique for each of us and yet we are all finding our way together. We also realize that the world religious traditions hold a part of the truth and the sacred writings throughout the world point the way.

Truth is being redefined. Instead of truth being the same forever, fixed and unchangeable, truth increases and refines itself as we grow and mature spiritually. Truth is not far off in the distance. It is something we live every day in the way we can recognize at that time. In this new way of being, truth is guided by compassion and forgiveness, listening to one another, and ridding ourselves of arrogance and self-righteousness.

In the new spirituality, a sense of the sacred is broadening and being seen in a new light. Sacredness is being liberated from physical buildings and moved back into the world, embracing all that has been left out. In the old paradigm of religion, nature is seen as a force to dominate. There is a feeling that we do not need to attend to our environment because the Rapture will take care of it all. And the body is rejected as sinful or bad and as lead-

*Action, like a sacrament, is the visible form of an invisible spirit, an outward manifestation of an inward power.* —Parker Palmer

ing us astray. In the new spirituality, the flesh no longer opposes the Spirit and the Spirit no longer stands against the flesh. The mystery behind life is that Spirit and matter are one in different forms. The Spirit enlivens the flesh and the flesh gives the Spirit a home. This is especially important to our next point.

*3. The reconnected mind and body contains its own innate wisdom.*
Wisdom and maturity manifest when you integrate the body with the mind with the Spirit. In the in-between world in the labyrinth, you are able to consciously connect them. This is why following your impulses is so important. It frees up the energy that would ordinarily be in the service of keeping you frozen and numbed to your experience.

But there are many levels to psychospiritual bodywork. Jung discovered the bridge between the atoms in matter and the archetypes in the psyche. There, an energetic arc of connection, a bandwidth—as the scientists may say—exists that communicates and is enlivened through myth and archetypes. Jung called this the "psychoid factor," but did not explore this further. Jungian analyst Marion Woodman has focused her life's work around this connection. Through dance and using the voice, dream work, didactic sessions, and

 *Do not wait for leaders; do it alone, person to person.* —Author unknown

mask-making, her work strengthens this connection between the body and the creative forces in our lives. Through this connection, healing can occur, and creative leaps in ones' lives are accomplished with greater ease. Visions can be brought into reality on the earth.

Fred Mitouer, in an article titled "Invoking the Mythos of the Emerging Human Species," offers the thesis that though we say we want peace, we fear that it would be boring. We are addicted to a "hyper-arousal that constant conflict breeds."[2] We must break through this addiction to energy streaming through us and slow down to a natural pace. This is hard work, but any activity that combines body movement with a flowing mind can break through these addictive energies that keep us divorced from ourselves, and from community as well. The labyrinth is an effective place to do this work. As we go through the portal to the imaginal realms, we find the thread of this connection. And as the labyrinth teaches us, we must experience our experience, or life will pass us by and we will feel empty and regretful at the end of it.

### 4. There are dangers on the path.

Living a spiritual life has embedded within it a natural joy that appears from time to time. During difficult times, it offers a solidarity and sureness even during the steep parts of the path. But if we do not take seriously what living a life in the Spirit entails, we can lose our way.

Choosing our own spiritual path leaves a lot of room for improvisation. We can choose those methods and teachings that support our inner transformation. But our picking and choosing also leaves us open to a "been there, done that" approach to spirituality. If we gather many different teachings from many different sources and glue them together without integrating them, it can lead to an empty, superficial approach.

I like the quality that Elizabeth Lesser has articulated: that we must be fearless in the examination of all that living on this earth means. We hope to look life straight in the eye and not avoid the fact that from time to time it is a "vale of tears." We hope to look death straight in the face and be ready to give way to it when the time comes. We attempt to be open to the magic and magnificence of each moment that we live, being fully present and mindful that there is mystery behind all life; and our assignment is to be open to it as best we can. We must be responsible for the unhealed parts of ourselves and be accountable as to how they hurt us and those we love.

One of the gravest dangers that can happen during this age of fear and despair is to make our own God. "Dear ones," says the Sufi teacher Hafiz, "beware of the tiny gods frightened men create to bring an anesthetic relief to their sad days." Unfortunately, creating God in our own image is easy to do if we do not follow an open-ended practice to support our spiritual life. The simple fact that many of us start out hearing the word "father" to describe God is fraught with the possibility of blending our earthly father, for good or ill, with the one in a supposed heaven.

Tom Picton, prominent in the Recovery movement, offers a litmus test as to whether we are creating God in our own image. He says: "You are creating God in your own image if the God you believe in hates the same people you do." There is much to think about in this quote. If our God is a hateful God that supports our own nastiness and small-mindedness, then it is time to find a guide and look within.

In the introduction, I offered the image of the labyrinth being a form of the Grail. The Grail meets you where you are, gives you what you need, and forms an "invisible web of relationships that connects individual destiny to service of others and to the earth, thereby granting meaning."[3] In the story, Parzival sees the Holy Grail during his first time in the Grail Castle. The Queen, dressed in silk finery and emanating with a soft light, carries the Grail placed on a dark green cloth into the feast. Each person at the feast steps before the Grail to receive from it the food and drink they most desire. "Its delights were very like what we are told of the kingdom of heaven."[4]

The Grail is symbolized many ways in these stories. Sometimes it is a stone, other times a jewel. After the stories were Christianized, the Grail was the cup into which the blood of Christ flowed at the crucifixion. In the Eschenbach version we have been using, the Grail is a cornucopia of abundance that flows with generosity to all who stand before it.

Imagine if we could be open to the abundance of the Spirit in our lives. Imagine how the citizens of the world would behave if each of us knew that there was enough to go around: food, oil, water, and money. But we must find our way to the Grail Castle. We must find our way out of the struggles with the ego into the imaginal realm. We must carry our questions within our hearts, be nurtured by beauty, accept that some suffering in life is inevitable, and allow ourselves to be present to receive the Mystery we call life.

Find your way to a labyrinth. It is a crucible of change, a watering hole for the Spirit, a tool for manifestation, a mirror of the soul, a path of prayer, a beacon of light, and a crucible for commuity. It is a place where we who are walking the Path can recognize one another.

# Notes

INTRODUCTION

1   Linda Sussman, *The Speech of the Grail: A Journey toward Speaking That Heals and Transforms* (New York: Lindisfarne Books, 1995), p. 1.

2   Archetypal labyrinths are ones that have been created anonymously and perfected over time through a collective spiritual tradition that has been passed down through the ages. For a fuller explanation, refer to the epilogue in the second edition of *Walking a Scared Path*. Original source, see Hermann Kern's *Through the Labyrinth* (New York: Prestel, 2001), p. 305.

3   In *Walking a Sacred Path*, I referred to this pattern as purgation, illumination, and union in keeping with the Christian mystical language of Teresa of Avila.

4   Sig Lonegren, for example, teaches a problem-solving method, using written questions placed on the turns of the path. However, since I do not use this method—it feels too prescribed for the work I am doing—I do not include it here.

5   Robert Sardello, *Facing the World with Soul, The Reimagination of Modern Life* (Hudson, NY: Lindisfarne Press, 1992), p. 182.

PART ONE: THE PRACTICE OF WALKING THE LABYRINTH

1   Anthony de Mello. *Writings Selected with an Introduction by William Dych, S. J.* Modern Masters Series (Maryknoll, NY: Orbis Books), p. 46.

2   C. G. Jung, *Nietzsche's Zarathustra: Notes of the Seminar Given in 1934 to 1939 by C. G. Jung,* Bollingen Series XCIX (Princeton, NJ: Princeton University Press, 1988), p. 237.

CHAPTER 1: FOUR GUIDELINES TO GAUGE YOUR SPIRITUAL GROWTH

1   D. H. Lawrence, "The Escape," *Kangaroo* (Cambridge: Cambridge University Press, 2000).

CHAPTER 2: LESSONS OF THE LABYRINTH

1   Dr. Keith Critchlow is an internationally known lecturer, teacher, and author. His many books include *Order in Space, Time Stands Still,* and *Islamic Patterns: An Analytical and Cosmological Approach.* This is a quote from one of his lectures.

2   Sylvia Shaindel Senensky, *Healing and Empowering the Feminine: A Labyrinth Journey* (Wilmette IL: Chiron Publications, 2003), p. 29.

CHAPTER 3: THE ART OF LABYRINTH WALKING

1  Matthew Fox, *Original Blessing: A Primer in Creation Spirituality Presented in Four Paths, Twenty-Six Themes, and Two Questions* (New York: Tarcher, 2000). For a direct application to the labyrinth see Georgiana Lofty, *Walking the Labyrinth: A Spiritual Journey through the Four Paths*, Doctoral Dissertation, University of Creation Spirituality (Oakland, CA, 2001).

2  To see a Finger Meditation Tool, go to www.Veriditas.org.


PART TWO: SPECIFIC USES FOR HEALING AND TRANSFORMATION

CHAPTER 5: START WHERE YOU ARE

1  When creating their labyrinth, the children in a Santa Fe public school put a large, flat stone at the entryway and called it the "pause stone."

CHAPTER 6: HEALING

1  The original source to encourage my thinking is Elfie Hinterkopf's book *Integrating Spirituality in Counseling: A Manual for Using the Experiential Focusing Method,* American Counseling Association (Alexandria, VA, 2004).

CHAPTER 7: SHADOW WORK

1  Frances Vaughn and Roger Walsh, Editors, *Accept This Gift*: *Selections from a Course in Miracles* (New York: Tarcher, 1983), p. 29.

CHAPTER 8: SOUL ASSIGNMENT

1  Jean Houston, *The Search for the Beloved*: *Journeys in Sacred Psychology* (New York: Tarcher, 1987), pp. 31–34.

2  James Hillman, *The Soul's Code: In Search of Character and Calling* (New York: Random House, 1996).

CONCLUSION: A SPIRITUALITY FOR OUR TIMES

1  Elizabeth Lesser, *A New American Spirituality: A Seeker's Guide* (New York: Random House, 2003), p. 38.

2  Fred Mitouer, "Taming the Dragons: The Biochemistry of Transformation," *Healing the Heart of the World* (Santa Rosa, CA: Elite Press, 2005).

3  Linda Sussman, *The Speech of the Grail: A Journey toward Speaking That Heals and Transforms* (New York: Lindisfarne Books, 1995), p. 1.

4  Wolfram von Eschenbach, *Parzival*, Book V, trans. Helen M. Mustard and Charles E. Passage (New York: Vintage, 1961), p. 238.